AFFAIRS OF THE HEART, SOUL, AND SPIRIT

By Margaret Blanchard

Published By
Milligan Books

Typesetting and Formatting
Margaret Blanchard

Cover Design By
Icehill MultiMedia

i

Published and Distributed by:
Milligan Books
an imprint of Professional Business Consultants
1425 W. Manchester, Suite B,
Los Angeles, California 90047
(213) 750-3592

First Printing, January 1998
10 9 8 7 6 5 4 3 2 1

ISBN 1-881524-48-5

Printed in the United States of America

Desprately, helplessly, longingly I cried
Quetly, patiently, lovingly God replied.
I pled and wept for a clue of my fate.
And the Master so gently said, "Child, you must wait."

Then quietly, softly, I learned my fate
as my Master replied once again, "You must wait."
So, I slumped in my chair, trying not to vacillate.
As I grumbled to myself, "Again? I have to wait?".

He said, the glow of my comfort late into the night.
The love and faith that I give you when you lose sight.
And though oft' my answers may seem terribly late.
my most precious answer of all is still, wait.

I want you to know what it means to live free.
And what I mean about "My grace is sufficient for thee."
I want you to know that I can save you, for a start
And for you to know the depth of the beat of my heart.

Author unknown

Dedication

This book is dedicated to the memory of my parents, the late Royal and Mary Jones. They were instrumental in my writing this book in so many ways. They provided my siblings and me with a firm foundation in our early beginnings in Memphis, Tennessee, on which we could build and maintain reasonable, sound, loving relationships with friends and other associates. The principles that came from their nurturing and discipline gave us an integrity that was not easy to abandon.

Acknowledgments

Affairs of the Heart, Soul and Spirit owes its life to many people who will not be named personally but I cannot, in good conscious, leave them out. Many people shared experiences from their personal lives and permitted me to share them with you. Those experiences became an invaluable part of this book. To all the contributors, I take this time to pay special tribute to each of you. My deepest, most sincere expressions of thanks to you all.

Of course it would be unscrupulous of me not to mention one of my most valued supporters, my husband, Larry Blanchard. His generosity with his time, energy, resources and unwavering confidence made my task much, much easier. He provided me with a new personal experience which I drew on while writing this book. I would also like to thank him for his laborious efforts in advertising and distributing my previous work, *The Birth of a Christian*.

I would like to pay a very special tribute to my sisters, Hardy, R.V., Mary, Sadie, my only brother Albert, as well as Mamie and Crissy who are now deceased. Along with a few special nieces and nephews, my siblings provided me with first hand experiences in sharing interests, activities and purposes.

My friend, prayer partner and sister by choice, Lisa Artis listened to all my numerous beginnings and offered very valuable advice and in-put every step of the way.

Author's Preface

Affairs of the Heart, Soul, and Spirit was not an easy book for me to write. I began many times and tried to write about what I thought readers wanted . Writing a book about relationships was a humungous task because relationships are so personal and private. I was certain, after a while, that I was not the person to do this but the idea continued to eat away at my innermost being. Seemingly, more people began to tell me things about their relationships or the road blocks they encountered when they tried to establish workable relationships.

I began to pray about it and hoped against hope that I would not be the one to write such a book. Seemingly, the more I prayed the more the idea burned within me. I began to talk with people and poll some readers. Everyone seemed excited about the idea. One day I was in Memphis, Tennessee at a book signing event when two young men in their late twenties, came over to my table and began to read the back cover of my book, *The Birth Of A Christian.* They seemed especially interested in the Publisher, Dr. Rosie Milligan's, statement, "How listening to the Holy Spirit led her to the meeting and marrying of her soul mate." They began to talk to me about their relationships. Finally one of them asked me, "Why don't you write a book on relationships?" I took that as confirmation that perhaps I was the one to write such a book. I began to seriously think more about relationships. I was surprised to find how much I did not know about establishing and maintaining wholesome relationships. I compiled the information and added some personal life experiences, both good and bad, and even did a comparative analysis dealing with the past and present. This, along with some inspiration, went into the writing of this book.

There are many different types of relationships that require different types of mind sets. This book will be about general relationships, with a few types added to clarify some points. However, most of the information can be applied to any type of relationship.

Affairs of the Heart, Soul, and Spirit will contain many real life experiences from real people. The names of most of the contributors will be changed in an effort to protect their privacy. Some contributors insisted that their names be used (Lisa Artis). Only those who insisted on their real names being used will be entered. The contributors willingly permitted me to use their experiences in an effort to lend some insight to readers. I have also used some of my own personal experiences, as well as some of the *"people experiences"* I gained as a long time health care professional. Some of the personal experiences may be similar to events that some readers have already encountered. I will rely on a proverb from one of the wisest men of all times to explain the possible similarities. King Solomon indicated that there is nothing new under the sun. *Whatever is has already been, and what will be has been before* (Ec. 3:15). It may be comforting to some readers to know that whatever they may be going through right now, others have encountered similar experiences. Remember, nothing is new.

Prologue

Affairs of the Heart, Soul and Spirit is the first in a series of books about various types of relationships. It opens with one of the most important relationships a person will ever enter into. Although this is not one's first relationship, it is the first one that a person decides for him/herself to establish. The most important relationship anyone can decide to enter into is a relationship with God, the Creator of mankind *Affairs of the Heart, Soul, and Spirit* is about the pivotal role one's inward qualities play in defining the total person. Some of the functions of these inward qualities will be discussed, as well as how they relate to self-definition.

This book is also about the elements of a reasonable, healthy relationship. It encourages readers to explore and compare some of these elements of reasonable, healthy relationships to their own characteristic traits as well as to the characteristic traits of their prospective associates. These elements should be reviewed *before* making a decision to enter into a very close relationship with anyone. Hopefully, some of the questions about why people respond and behave in certain ways will be answered. The foundation for all future relationships will be visited and the emotional health, or lack of it in the lives of many people will be discussed. There will also be information on emotional injuries and healing, boundaries and bondage, and other characteristic traits that numerous people exhibit.

The ending of the book will give readers some insights on *the* most important relationship anyone could ever enter into. The epilogue will give a brief synopsis of the types of relationships that the next book will discuss specifically.

Some of the major purposes for writing such a book include, empowering readers with some general knowledge about relationships and lending some seemingly, forgotten ideas on approaching new relationships. The writer wants to assure readers that they have choices and to encourage them not to make hasty decisions. The poems at the beginning of each chapter [by the author] express that theme throughout the book. In any relationship people will be expected to share some of life's most precious assets. It is of paramount importance for the readers to fully understand what they are endeavoring to share, and who they are about to share their *valuables* with.

The information within this book can be used to enhance any existing relationship as well as lend assistance in establishing new relationships. References to God, the Spirit and quotations from the Bible will be found throughout this book. To readers who may not be familiar with things of the Spirit, a more qualitative concept of Spiritual matters will be discussed in the last chapter of the book.

AFFAIRS OF THE HEART, SOUL, AND SPIRIT

CONTENTS

Chapter One

UP CLOSE AND PERSONAL

Be silent my child, and you will see,
that you should take some time to get to know "thee"
Before you begin to think that fulfillment is not your fate
know that you have the time and the patience to wait.

It is the nature of people to have a desire to interact with each other on a continuous basis. Some interactions are productive and others are counter-productive. Both may stimulate people to enter into some type of relationship with each other. Relationships of any type on any level between people who are in control of their affairs are the results of decisions they make. Whether the relationships will be productive or counter-productive will depend on the type of materials individuals are working with. There is much more to establishing and maintaining wholesome, healthy relationships than incidental associations or spastic interactions. The foundation of each relationship has to be established and the quality of the building materials put to the test before a relationship can receive the seal that identifies it as healthy, wholesome and functional.

Relationships between human beings involves people. All human beings have many things in common, but because of

1

their abilities to think and make decisions they, along with other unique qualities, have differences that can separate them. People have different ideas about what a relationship is. Some people cannot differentiate between a healthy relationship and an unhealthy one. Unfortunately people do not always conform to the standards that have been pre-determined and proven to be effective. Because people are uniquely different from each other in numerous ways, it is very important for everyone to gain a working knowledge of what makes relationships healthy and wholesome. Everyone should know some of the things that differentiates a reasonable relationship from an unreasonable one. It is often essential for people to get up close and personal with others before making a decision to enter into certain types of relationships. The very first person anyone should get up close and personal with is themselves. It is vital for people to take the time and exert the energy getting to know themselves. Before attempting to establishing relationships with others, everyone should ask and answer the following: Who am I? What do I really want? How will I achieve my goals in certain relationships? Meditate on each question before attempting to answer any of them. Knowing who you are can make an enormous difference in what you will accept and what you will reject as you ponder over new relationships. It can also be helpful in determining how you should be functioning in your existing relationships.

Good, wholesome, healthy relationships involve spending quality time getting to know the people that you choose to interact with. People establish relationships for many reasons but mostly to enjoy the companionship of others with whom they share common interests. Rarely does anyone set out to establish superficial relationships that are not grounded and cannot grow roots deep enough to facilitate progressive development. People generally want to know each other. They want to interact on numerous levels. They want to get inside the heads of those with whom they share portions of their lives. It takes time, energy and effort to really get to know anyone. It is crucial for people who intend to accompany each other, or share things in common with each other, and form a camaraderie, to get beyond the superficial phase as quickly as possible. The best way to really get to know what others are interested in and what motivates them to respond in certain ways is through a constant exchange of information.

Many important characteristic traits are revealed in casual conversations. There are those who believe there has to be an attracting feature or a "calling card" to get the attention of others initially. That may be true in some cases. External appearances may be enough to attract someone's attention initially, but outward appearances will never be enough to nourish a growing relationship. Outward appearances can be very deceiving. It is what is on the inside of a person's heart, spirit, soul, and mind that truly defines that person.

Pay special attention to how a person defines him/herself. Numerous people define themselves by external features, professional appointments, educational achievements, or social status. There are masses of unhappy people who proudly define themselves by titles that give the appearance of success.

There may be an equal number of happy and unhappy people who reluctantly define themselves as "only a laborer" or other roles that do not scream success. Success is the major goal in numerous people's lives. Their idea of success is what motivates them to enter into many relationships. So the things that define success to them are the things that become priorities. Different people measure success by different standards. Some believe they are successful when they have acquired enough material assets to live comfortably and duly impress their colleagues and peers. Other people, who are goal orientated, define success as reaching their self-prescribed goals. There are a select few who believe that they have achieved success when they have reached a state of peace, harmony and eternal joy that cannot be shaken by things in the material world. How people perceive success is directly related to how they feel about themselves. There are those who do not believe success or *fulfillment is their fate* because they are measuring success by someone else's yardstick.

Once a person begin to look at themselves from the inside out he/she may get a different view of who really dwells inside.

Getting to know someone means making decisions about sharing one's space and entering into the space of someone else. This includes the sharing of some secrets and maybe portions of lifestyles. People usually decide beforehand how much of their space they are willing to give up and how much of themselves they intend to share with others. People decide which habits they want to expose and what lifestyle they intend to present to others. There are some suspicious people who want to wait until they have acquired a body of information about others before they share anything creditable or of importance about themselves. Because most people have dark sides, fears and anxieties, they are inquisitive about what they believe others are hiding or holding back. Those same people usually have no intentions of exposing their own character flaws or imperfections.

Numerous people have a tendency to identify themselves by the reflections they see in the mirror. They habitually focus on what they think is lacking in their appearance. What they believe they lack physically often have a profound affect on their personalities. They are never quite satisfied with what the reflection they see in the mirror. They are forever trying to make themselves over, believing that this will make them a better person. Most people are overly critical of themselves. Very few people take the time or exert the energy necessary to really get to know the person who dwells within their body, especially if they are overly concerned about their image. The real person in each of us can only be found within our heart, soul, and spirit. This is the person that is rarely exposed. A person's social friends, intimate friends and other associates speak volumes about who a person really is. The old adage, "Birds of a feather flock together," may be pregnant with treasures of wisdom. People who share common interests, activities and purpose, also seem to share a mental connection of some sort. They seem to be drawn to each other naturally.

The universe is filled with people who have misconceptions about who they really are. Their identification of themselves is representative of who they want to be or who others think they should be. Some people have traits that they view as flaws because they are different from their peers. They spend quality time trying to hide or cover-up these traits. I once knew a very beautiful young woman who continuously pressed her lips together very tightly. Some people actually thought she was grimacing. She had been told by her mother that her full lips were unattractive. She believed that if she never revealed her lips no one would ever notice their fullness. Actually her lips were one of her most attractive features, but the idea of unattractiveness had been instilled in her as a young child. She attempted to conceal one of the features that made her attractive. There is no end to the number of people who think the things that they attempt to conceal are too ugly or too painful to be exposed.

Since it is important for most people to be liked and accepted by their peers and associates, they quench good qualities within themselves that they deem unacceptable, unimpressive or unattractive. People seem to be so concerned about what others think of them until they fail to nurture some of their most unique, useful qualities. Many times they become so good at suppressing portions of themselves that they begin to believe some of their unattractive qualities cease to exist. They often build entirely different people within their own minds, based on wishful thinking. The only problem with that is, the qualities they seem to concealed in the darkest corners of the mind do not go away. Late at night when the whole world seems to be asleep, the hidden qualities come back to haunt them. Dreams and nightmares will often bring them to the surface of the conscious mind again. There seems to be a constant battle going on within that person. The inner person always seems to be struggling to get out and the outer person fights to keep that person hidden. This causes a person to continuously look for new and different ways to conceal their flaws while their inner qualities struggle for exposure. There may be many ways of dealing with the struggle. First one has to acknowledge that faults, fears and frustrations exist within his/her innermost being. Once the confess has taken place, he/she is free to bring them out in the open and begin to deal with them. After all, the most important people (you and God) already know all about every aspect of you. When one exercises the freedom of admitting that they are human beings with human faults, some of their imperfections may not seem as unattractive as they thought they were. It may be that they only appeared to be unattractive because they were being compared to the qualities of someone else. Whenever anyone compares any of their God-given qualities to those of someone else, they will never measure up. Self-assessment was meant to be personal, not comparative. Each individual should take a close look at themselves through the eyes of their Creator.

God, in His infinite wisdom, took particular care in creating you to be unique. You will never become like someone else or be measured correctly by someone else's calibrations. You were designed with specifications that separate you from anyone else on the face of the earth. Your inner qualities are part of a personal design suited for you exclusively. Some of the qualities you may be trying to hide or eliminate could be essential to who you were created to be. Once you have gained enough courage to expose them, you may learn to accept them. The choices you make for your livelihood and your lifestyle do not adequately represent you. The choices people make are separate from their 'person.' Some people choose to work as engineers, carpenters, teachers physicians, lawyers, or any number of things. Failure to make good, profitable choices may cause people to do things that they do not want to do. No choice is a decision to accept things that one does not want to accept. People are usually very proud to say, "I am a doctor, lawyer or an Indian Chief." Does this mean if you can no longer practice in your chosen profession that you cease to exist? You are not integrated or blended into the choices you make.

Your choices are only extensions of what you do. You can and will exist outside of your choices. You are so much more than any of those things that you decided to do. It is not always easy to focus on the person God created you to be. In reality, you have dimensions, feelings, ideas, and areas within your heart, soul, and spirit that you probably have never taken the time to discover!

So very many things are factored into defining one individual. While anatomically and functionally, people may seem to be similar, there are some things within each person that identifies him/her as separate from anyone else. Your "fingerprints" within your inner person will not match the "fingerprints" of anyone else. That is how special you are. So, before attempting to get to know anyone else, you should, *"Be silent my child so that you can see, that God intended for you to know the one you live with, and the one you call me."* You are probably grossly familiar with your physical attributes. You see the exterior portion of yourself every time you look in the mirror. Now is the perfect time to begin to familiarize yourself with the real you, that person who lives within. Make a decision, establish a plan and discipline yourself to enter into a very personal relationship with your self. This may be one of the most important relationships you will ever establish. To learn some valuable information about establishing such a relationship, I would like to invite you to take an exciting, cleansing, fulfilling journey of self-discovery. This journey can take you into the depths of the innermost chambers of your being. It is exceedingly important for you to take this journey alone, and for you to take special care to enter into a relationship with the real person that God created you to be and not the one you wish you were. I have a few important comments before you begin your journey.

Make sure you are prepared, mentally, spiritually and emotionally to take this journey. Honest self-exploration is not always easy. This journey should have a specific, defined purpose that can become beneficial to you. Remember, almost everything that has happened, is happening right now and will happen in the future are the end results of some decision that you have made as an adult, or a decision you will make in the future. Even the lack of decision making will also affect your life as it is today. There are many things that happened in childhood that were not under the control of the now-adult. You do not have to remain in bondage to those things that adversely affect you as an adult. You only have to acknowledge their existence and how they affect the now-adult. So, begin your journey by *deciding* to take full responsibility for all of your *decisions*. You must let your guard down if you want the journey to be profitable to you. Make a real solemn pledge to yourself to be completely and blatantly honest about all of your discoveries. You are not trying to prove anything to anyone else on this journey. There will be no one on this journey for you to impress. Whatever you discover along the way, authenticate and accept it for what it really is. Call it by its name, no matter how wonderful or distasteful it seems to be. You do not have to be afraid or ashamed of what anyone will think of you on this journey. Whatever you do, please do not attempt to rationalize it away or justify its existence if you find it distasteful. If it is something positive, embrace it, make sure it is in fertile soil, nurture it and give it room to grow. If it is negative, look for its origin. Once you find the source you do not have to let it remain within you. You can dig it up, roots and all, and cast it out without leaving a trace of its former existence. You may need some help when it comes to casting things out of your heart, soul, and spirit. Supernatural help is available to you, which may be what you need if the adversary has strongholds on your inner qualities. People from all walks of life may be dominated by the adversary in some area of their lives. They take the body that God created and radically alter it, rendering it imperfect, by piercing it and permanently drawing on parts of the body God created in perfection according to His standards. Many people do not realize that self-mutilation is a form of disobedience to God. It is impossible for anyone to fight against the adversary in their own power. When you are influenceed by the Holy Spirit, the weapons of choice you use to do battle with the adversary are not worldly, *but mighty through God to the pulling down of strongholds; casting down imaginations and every high thing that elevates itself against*

10

the knowledge of God and bring into captivity every thought to the obedience of Christ (II Cor. 10:4-5 paraphrased). You should not only want to cast out the qualities that are not part of the person God created you to be, but you should seek divine help in demolishing everything that sets itself up against the knowledge of God. Sometimes the (demon) spirits of the air are instrumental in building strongholds within your inner being about anything. You must not permit this to happen. This is why it is important to replace all of your negative attributes with positive ones immediately. Failure to fill your empty spaces with something positive could result in their becoming occupied with more negative attributes than you started out with. *When an evil spirit comes out of a man, it goes through arid places seeking rest and does not find it. Then it says, "I will return to the house I left." When it arrives, it finds the house unoccupied, swept clean and in order. Then it goes and takes with it seven other spirits more wicked than itself, and they go in and live there. And the final condition of that person is worse than the first*(Mat. 12:43-45). These evil spirits want to make sure they fortify the strong holds they set up within a person. I cannot over-express the importance of replacing all of your negative attributes with positive ones immediately. You must make a decision, create a plan and discipline yourself to follow the plan to become positive in your thoughts as well as your actions.

Unless you are diligent about being the best that you can be, your self-discovery journey will a counter-productive tour.

You must believe that you are important to God and theorefore

11

important to yourself, before you can feel like you are important to anyone else.

If you find yourself comparing your qualities and attributes to those of someone else, stop and take a break before continuing on. Once you have begun the journey, you must remain committed to finishing it for your own sake. Do not allow anyone or anything to convince you to abandon your self-discovery journey until you are satisfied that you know who you are and have a good idea of where you want to go and how you intend to get there.

Remember, this is personal, something that you are doing for you. Your entire future could depend upon effectively completing this journey. Do not overwhelm yourself by thinking about what the entire trip will entail, or clutter your mind with thoughts of, "what will happen if......" Just take the trip one day and one step at a time. Move at your own pace, stopping to take a break whenever you become overwhelmed.

Many, many people do not believe that they have a valid identity that defines them as a productive, purposeful person. You may need to take this trip so that you can define who you are and become more familiar with the good qualities that you possess. People who have never taken a self-discovery journey spend so much of their precious time trying to be someone that other people want them to be. Perhaps they did not get to choose their own professions and fulfill their own purpose and they feel trapped into the person that someone else decided that they should be. Others are forever in a state of becoming someone that they perceive as important and/or successful. They imitate the traits of others and try to walk in shoes that do not fit them well. It is awfully hard to keep in step with someone who is walking to the beat of his own heart. Trying to keep step to the beat of someone else's heart can prevent you from hearing the beat of your own heart. Once you make a decision to shut out all of the external noise and become quiet enough to hear your own heart beat, and begin to step to your own heart beat, you will probably experience a sudden rush of freedom. Feel free to say; "At last I have come to a place of self-acceptance." Trying to fit into someone else's shoes or trying to keep pace with someone else's heart beat is a form of bondage. Never, never be afraid or embarrassed to admit that you are different and the pace that you are keeping in step with may be different. You were created to be different. Different is neither bad nor good. It is just distinct and separate from everyone else. Everyone else is different from you by design. They may not want to admit it because it may be popular not to be like everyone else, but please believe that everyone is different by design too. While you are focusing on someone else's qualities and attributes with admiration, someone may be looking at you with sincere admiration. So, do not be so quick to cast out any of your qualities until you are satisfied that they do not belong within your being. Seriously ask yourself if things you find distasteful are intricate parts of who you are or who you are to become. Ask yourself: "Who are they distasteful to?" Examine your reasons for finding things distasteful. Do not try to be like anyone else. Work towards being a better you. You alone can improve, embrace, reject and/or cast out qualities within yourself. It is very tiring trying to be you and someone else too! It may be nice to know that no one alive is perfect. While your goal may be to reach perfection, you will never reach that status as long as you are alive in the flesh. However, putting forth the effort can be so productive.

Once you get inside your inner chambers, make sure you explore every nook and cranny. Expose all your secret hiding places. Bring absolutely everything out in the open. There is no one around to judge or condemn you. You are on this journey alone. If you have tucked away your fears and even your deepest, darkest secrets, now is the time to bring them out and dispose of anything that prevents you from being all that you can be. You alone may know what you have hidden. It may be a good idea to write down the things that you have been hiding for years. Once you feel confident enough to share some of your fears, anxieties and flaws with a trusted friend you should confess them and wait for the relief to come.

Therefore confess your sins [faults] to each other and pray for each other so that you may be healed(Jas. 5:16). Hiding things that we know are wrong and unjust and trying to justify doing so is a natural response for all human beings. Everyone probably inherited traits from their ancestors, and humans inherited those traits from the first family. *The man and his wife heard the sound of the Lord God walking in the garden in the cool of the day, and they hid from the Lord God among the trees of the garden. But the Lord God called to the man, "Where are you?" He answered, "I heard You in the garden because I was naked [or exposed]; so I hid*(Gen. 3:8-10)." The first born son, Cain, of the first family also did something unacceptable. He killed his brother and buried him in an effort to cover up his deeds. When the Lord said to Cain, *where is your brother Abel?* Cain added lying to his misdeeds. He answered, *I don't know.* Nothing you suppress or cover-up or hide is hidden from the Lord God. The Lord replied,*"Listen! Your brother's blood cries out to me from the grave"*(Gen. 4: 4:9-10). These are definitely not admirable, acceptable traits. The consequences were very great in each case. There will also be consequences in accordance with your misdeeds when you hide, cover-up or lie about the outcome of the some of decisions that you have made. Some things may have been hidden so long that even you may not be sure of what you will discover. People like to think of themselves as good or "normal." That is why they attempt to justify, rationalize or cover-up their misdeeds. But you must let it all hang out on this journey. Do not try to hide anything from yourself. If you cannot be honest with yourself you will have problems being honest with anyone else. It is a very bad place to be in when you know that you are practicing deception, even if no one else knows it. Remember, the relationship that you are developing now will last forever. Once you have confessed, exposed, cast out and replaced the qualities and traits that kept you in bondage, living with yourself will become much more pleasant. You should be aiming at the ability to look in the mirror and say to the entire person staring back at you, "I really like you and I am growing to love you more each day."

This is not a turn-around trip or a week-end escapade. It is a compelling process that could take a very long time. If you intend to truly establish a relationship based on trust, honesty, loyalty, commitment and respect with the real person that goes beyond your exterior, you must decide that this journey is important enough to spend quality time on. How you establish and keep this relationship up will have an affect on every other relationship you enter into for the remainder of your life. Knowing who you are and what makes you tick can give valuable insight into why you behave the way you do. It may hold the key to some of your successes and failures in certain areas of your life. Just knowing some answers to some of your "Why me?" questions may have unlimited possibilities.

I am sure you must be wondering "when will this journey begin and when can I go aboard?" Only you can decide the when and where. I can give some insight into the how. There may never be a better time than right now nor a better place than wherever you are right now. This entire adventure involves you. You might begin by making your own decision and taking full responsibility for whatever you choose to do. You may have a lot of excess baggage to lose but I guarantee you will gain more than you lose.

You can begin by empowering yourself with as much knowledge as possible about what defines you. I will attempt to assist by giving some general insights on self-identification or definition, but it will be up to you to define the person you discover. This will not be an anatomy and physiology type of review. It is a realistic view of the inner make up of human beings. It will be all about character, emotions, feelings, perceptions, impressions and motivations. The journey begins by exploring some of the things that control and influence you. Climb aboard!

Let us begin at the heart of the matter. Almost everyone understands that the heart is the blood pumping organ that is vital to the physical life of all human beings. However, the heart is much more than that. It plays a central role in the personality development, intellectual responses, and some of the inner qualities that dictate the way you behave. Those inner qualities include the way you feel about certain things, what affects your moods, your natural desires and spiritual desires to respond to certain types of stimulus. Your inner qualities are responsible for "directing the traffic" in relationship to what you see, what you believe and what you think. These qualities interpret what you see and how you believe and the impressions you form on a continuous basis. The center of emotions arises from somewhere within the heart. The emotions control many of your conscious qualities such as feelings, moods and passions. Within the untouchable, complex system of the emotions, you are motivated to respond to things in accordance with your personal impressions without regard to the rhyme or reason of anyone else. Fear and love are also identified as emotional feelings. People fear things that seem real to them whether they are real to anyone else or not. They respond to their impressions of things that are real in their minds, although the things they perceive as real may not actually exist. The body is put on notice that something is threatening your well-being. It prepares to fight or run in response to your impression. I remember a classic example of response to an impression that had nothing to substantiate it in the real world.

Megan Brown was a young girl about eight or nine years

old. She was in the process of recovering from a chronic illness and was instructed to rest in bed most of the time. Her friends, peers, and neighbors had brought her many gifts, including fruit baskets, toys and money. She kept her things on top of a chest of drawers at the head of her bed. She had sisters close to her age who occasionally asked her to share her gifts with them. Megan often used her gifts to bait her sisters into spending time with her in the bedroom. Sometimes it worked and sometimes it didn't.

One day Megan was in the room alone while the rest of the family was in the living room laughing, talking and enjoying each other's company. Megan felt lonely and isolated. She wanted to join her family but was restricted to her bed. Her niece Tina, who was about three or four, passed by Megan's bed on her way to the bathroom. When Tina was returning to the living room to join the family, Megan enticed her to come and get in the bed with her so she could have some company. She gave Tina some fruit from her basket and promised to let her play with some of her new toys. Tina ate the fruit and played with the toys for a while and soon fell asleep. Megan *thought* she heard someone moving her things around on top of the chest of drawers. She could not see that area from her bed. She assumed it was her sisters. She yelled out, "Y'all better leave my things alone before I tell." It was quiet for a few minutes. Megan *thought* she heard someone at the head of her bed moving her things around on top of the chest of drawers again. This time she yelled out to her parents that her sisters were going into her things without permission. Her parents informed her that her sisters were not at home and had not been for quite some time. Megan was certain she heard someone. Her *impression* was, it must have been a ghost. She immediately became frightened and jumped from the bed and attempted to extract her niece Tina, who became entangled in the bed covers. Megan began to scream hysterically saying, that a ghost was in the room and it would not let go of Tina! Of course there was actually no ghost and Tina was merely entangled in the covers but Megan responded to her impression which had no existence in reality. She responded to what she perceived as real but only seemed real in her mind.

Everyone may have some views that are based on their personal feelings, which may or may not conform to reason. Now would be a good time to compare some of your personal impressions to things that actually exist. Some of your fears and anxieties may concern a few ghosts from your past that really do not exist in reality. There may be some things existing in your mind that could hinder you from being all that you can be, even though they are only *your* impressions. You might want to delve into the origin of your impressions to make sure you are not afraid of ghosts that do not exist in reality. Only you can make that decision and do an honest to goodness reality check into the things that seem to haunt you. Impressions can affect your moods, the trend of your thoughts, and your passions. Different people have different levels of perceptions and responses that correspond to their personal feelings, moods and passions. Your mood represents your state of mind at a given moment. Your inclinations, tempera-ment, attitude, nature and spirit are some of the things that are affected by your moods. Moods tend to change with new and different perceptions and impressions. You can change your moods by changing your attitude. Once you know and can acknowledge the truth, based on factual information about some things that you may have had unfounded impressions of in the past, you can make a decision to change your attitude and your responses. Any changes you decide to make must "feel" right to you. You are in the driver's seat here, you can table anything that you are not sure about. It might be a good idea to pick up a pencil and pad to take on this journey. Some of the things you may want to remember or go back and re-examine may be too important to commit to memory.

You may be emotionally affected by your surroundings, things that you have experienced, things you have vague or unreasonable impressions about, and/or things you need to deal with. How you feel about these things will dictate how you respond. Your feelings, moods and passions are interconnected. Passions are strong emotions that are not easily controlled. Love, happiness, hate, anger and greed are all expressions arising from your passions. All these qualities are part of a complex system known as the emotions. The emotions arise from an untouchable place within the heart. Sometimes people seem to think from the emotional center within their heart rather than from their intellectual center within the brain. The heart may have many more known and unknown functions. We may discover a few more of those functions as we continue this journey.

The heart is sometimes referred to as the *gut or the pit* although it may not have any digestive functions. Reference is also made to some form of intellectual distribution as another function of the heart. Understand that it is not one of the major responsibilities of the heart to acquire, process and distribute information, but the heart is believed to play a part in some of your thoughts and some of your reasons for responding to certain things. Thoughts are said to be made clear within the heart. It plays an intricate role in highlighting some of everyone's intellectual abilities. Sometimes people may think within their minds, that they cannot perform certain tasks. Their minds may dictate to them that they do not have the strength or the know how to do certain things. The heart may, on occasion, overrule the mind and give some people the "feeling within their heart" that they can perform the task. Some very serious considerations and meditations arise from within the heart. Some people respond to their thought reflections even when they have no concrete knowledge to substantiate their thoughts. Thought reflections are very real, and probably related to intuition in some way.

Intuition is defined as, the act of knowing without using the rational process. One has acute insight or is inspired through intuition. Inspiration can stimulate the emotions to a high level of activity or feeling. Inspirations also arise from within the heart. The Creator of mankind assures us, in the message he gave Isaiah to give to the people, that the heart is capable of understanding, ...*they might see with their eyes and hear with their ears and understand with their hearts and turn and be healed* (Is. 6:10). Some people just know within their hearts that they should do certain things beforehand. Sometimes their knowledge may be very limited in some areas but they believe that they can do some things if they just put forth their best efforts.

I can truly attest to my heart overruling my mind. On one particular occasion, I wanted to begin to use the Microsoft Word Program. At that time, I had not acquired nearly enough knowledge to become efficient enough to write a book! I was very concerned about my incapability. It is very hard for someone else to write for me because I am forever creating even as I correct errors. One night, following a fervent prayer for direction, after I had become frustrated with someone else's effort to assist me, I felt compelled to go downstairs to the computer. I knew how to turn it on and get into the program and that was about all! Within my heart I believed that I could do it if I just put forth an effort. Somewhere within my innermost being, I was inspired to make an attempt. When I followed the feeling within my heart without thinking about my lack of knowledge, I began to type in Microsoft and typed for three hours straight. I made many errors and found out how to correct many of them that night. When I finished I felt like I had made some right moves; I was even able to save my document until I was ready to get back to it again. Never fail to listen to your heart. You are the only one who can hear or reflect on the thoughts that arise from within your heart.

It is within the human heart where mankind can meet the word of God. *For it is with your heart that you believe and are justified....*(Ro. 10:10). The ability to make decisions that initiate actions is also within the heart. Your willpower or ability to exercise control, by deliberate purpose, over your impulses comes from within your heart. You make impulses comes from within the heart. You make use of your will to accept or reject God's word when it is met within the heart. Again, how you respond to the word of God depends upon your personal, private impression of Him and His word. The perceptions or impressions on which the heart reflects or meditates arises from the status of the heart and play a gigantic role in defining the whole person. The status of the human heart is either natural and unaltered or transformed through redemption (redemption will be explained more fully in chapter six). The reflections of the heart are made manifest in the deeds, actions and behavior of a person. *"What comes out of a man is what makes him unclean. For from within, out of men's hearts, come evil thoughts, slander, deceit, arrogance, and folly* (Mk. 7:21-22).

The heart alone does not control all the attitudes and behaviors of any individual; neither does it define a person completely. It is the spirit and attitude of oneness between the heart, soul, spirit and mind along with some inherited, environmental and learned traits, that define the total person. All the inward properties necessary for life are within the spirit. It is the spirit that gives and maintains life as well as defines the characteristics of living beings. The prevailing attitude, mental and moral condition of a person as well as his/her moods and tendencies are under the influence of his/her spirit. Sometimes *nature* and *spirit* are used inter-changeably. Basically they have some of the same functions. The nature of a person is consistent with his/her character. That nature is the controller or the major source of influence over how one behaves under certain conditions. The character of a person is a combination of his/her emotional, intellectual and moral properties. Your character is one of the major things that readily distinguishes you from anyone else.

Everyone was born with a sinful, natural, unaltered, undisguised nature that was inherited from the first family to whom everyone seems to be genetically related. That nature affects people's inclinations to conform to usual, ordinary things of nature. The things that people respond to naturally include all the observable, evident things within the material world. The material world is also called the realm of sin controlled by Satan, who is the ruler or prince of that realm of sin. Jesus acknowledged Satan as the prince of this world. *For the prince of this world is coming. He has no hold on me* (Jn. 14: 30). Satan only has influence over the people whose nature continues to remain in a fallen or natural state even though Jesus came and redeemed the world and all of the people who exercised control over their impulses or will to make a conscious decision to follow Him and His teachings. *God did not send His Son into the world to condemn the world, but to save the world through Him. Who ever believes in Him is not condemed* (Jn. 3:17-18). Beliefs involve attitude changes and other changes that take place within the heart, and spirit, of a person. No one alive is held accountable for the nature that he/she inherited but everyone will be held accountable for their decision to accept or reject the offer to receive a new Spiritual nature that will correspond to the nature of God. All human beings believe in something or someone. Some believe in God, some believe in themselves, others believe in a being that controls some of the occurrences

24

are very personal. Some people believe in many gods, or a single god who is limited in its abilities to perform or even gods who are inanimate. Again, it is a matter of personal decisions based on personal impressions, actual knowledge, and how people decide to apply the knowledge they have acquired, that influence their belief systems. Many of *your* basic activities, interests and life purposes are all intertwined within the status of your personal nature or spirit. It is what and who *you* believe in that influences your thought processes and your behavior. *Make a tree good and its fruit will be good, or make a tree bad and its fruit will be bad, for a tree is recognized by its fruit. The good man brings good things out of the good stored up in him and the evil man brings evil things out of the evil stored up in him. For out of the overflow of the heart the mouth speaks* (Mat.12:33-35). The Spirit of God influences people to store up good things in their hearts. The spirit of Satan is in direct opposition to God. He puts forth a great effort to influence people to store up evil within themselves. Your spirit is that force or source of power within that inspires your thought processes, your words, and your actions. It is the thing that keeps you moving and breathing and gives you vigor. It imparts courage and interests in specific things. Some of the things that you are inspired to do or say may be good or bad, depending upon who or what inspired you. Your spirit influences the mind to resolve itself to certain facts and impressions. It is a close affiliate of the mind, yet it is distinguished from the physical body in some of its functions. The soul is said to interact with the spirit. It is no material body or form. It functions as the disembodied spirit of human beings and is said to be immortal, which means that it is free and independent and can live forever.

The soul separates from the mortal body at death. In its disembodied (separated) state, the soul is still susceptible to happiness and misery according to the Scriptures. *The rich man also died and was buried. In hell, where he was tormented he looked up and saw Abraham far away. He called, have pity on me. I am in agony in this fire* (Lk. 16:22-24). The state of one's spirit at the time of their death will determine the future state of their disembodied soul. David, who understood that his disembodied soul would live on after his physical body had died, speaks of the future position of his soul to the Lord. *In Thy presence is the fullness of joy...there are pleasures evermore. For Thy will not leave my soul in hell...* (Psm. 16:11, 10 KJV). David expected his soul to be in the presence of the Lord, and not in hell where the souls of those who did not trust in God during their lifetime are appointed to spend eternity. He believed he had a right to expect this based on the condition of his heart, soul, and spirit as he responded in obedience to the principles of right, wrong, repentance, and forgiveness. The expressed conditions of his heart, soul, and spirit were made manifest in the way he treated everyone with whom he came in contact. The same will be true of you. How you relate to others in any type of relationship will be an expression of who you are on the inside.

Your nature/spirit/soul are all intricate parts of who you

really are as well as who you will become in the future. There are two major spiritual beings who influence every individual's behavior in many ways. One is the spirit of darkness who controls the material realm of sin. The other is the Spirit of light who controls the world including heaven and earth. God, who is the most powerful Spirit there is, even controls the dark, evil spirits, including the ruler of the material world. Satan whom Jesus refers to as the thief, and his demons, are organized against God and everything that is right. *The thief comes only to steal and kill and destroy; I have come that they may have life, and have it to the full,* says Jesus in John 10:10. The thief knows truth about who Jesus is and His purpose and plan for everyone's life. He knows that Jesus can set anyone free from the bondage that his influence holds them hostage to. He will do anything to prevent people from knowing the truth.

You may possess many of the fruits of the material world, but do you have peace, joy, and harmony within yourself? That is really what most relationships are about, filling in the empty spaces within. You are the only one who can make a decision about the present and future state of your soul. These are some things that you should probably take some special time to think very seriously about before making a hasty, on-the-spot decision. As far-fetched as some of this must sound to some people, it is based on truth. Always remember, the choices you make will affect the way you define yourself right now and who you will become in the future. You should take a moment to reflect upon the condition of your heart, soul, and spirit. Do you have that sense of unity within yourself? If there is conflict within, perhaps you need to make a decision. Whether you will decide that you want to develop to your fullest potential or not is up to you.

When your spiritual qualities are combined with your emotional, moral and intellectual qualities you will have many of the things necessary to define yourself in a nutshell. All of these inner properties are interrelated. Your moral qualities are made manifest by your concerns for the principles of right and wrong behavior as you interact with other people. People with good, moral character make it their business to know and follow whatever the laws are that governs acceptable behavior in any given situation. They readily accept standards that have been tried, tested and accepted by the moral majority. They have a conscious sense of what is just and unjust and put forth every effort to adhere to these standards. The moral character of a person arises from his/her belief systems, emotions and intellectual capabilities. People who are concerned about their reputation and their moral integrity usually approach life from a reasonable standpoint, within the boundaries of common sense. Whether a person is capable of performing within the boundaries of reason and common sense will depend upon his/her intellectual capabilities among other things.

Almost everyone is capable of acquiring, processing and applying knowledge. Acquisition of knowledge does not necessarily measure a person's intellect. There are other factors that determine the capacity of each individual's mind and how each person processes and applies knowledge. Whatever a person thinks, memorizes, perceives, feels, imagines and decides to do are in accordance with the way his or her mind functions. All of their life experiences, as well as their environmental, natural and spiritual inclinations are also factored in. The mind is one of the major control centers for the entire body. But, it cannot function independently of the other qualities, properties, attributes and characteristics that define a total person. Information is delivered into the mind in much the same way as data is entered into a computer. The way the mind processes information is based on an individual's ability to make judgments and reach conclusions. The mind reflects on, and responds to whatever information it has received and retained from one's past experiences.

An impression is formed, based on what is already stored in the mind and the data that is being acquired. Signals are transmitted to the necessary parts of the body to respond in accordance with the impression that the mind has formed. That response is in accordance with data in-put. The mind is not limited to the knowledge that has been acquired and its intuitions. However, whatever insights, intuitions or knowledge have been gained by perception, set the boundaries of one's wisdom and understanding. The level of a person's vulnerability to the information received determines how he/she will respond. People cannot respond beyond their knowledge, intuition or inspiration. Intellect, or the faculties of reasoning and knowing are distinctly different from the feelings that are associated with the heart. The mind does not necessarily seek out information; it absorbs what it receives through the senses. You can control many of the things that are retained within your mind. What kind of data are you acquiring? Does the data that you absorb bring you peace and harmony, or does it cause inner conflict and anxiety? There is no known limits to how much information the mind can retain.

It is not the quantity of knowledge that builds character. It is the quality of knowledge that makes the difference.

Many people define themselves by the amount of knowledge they have acquired in certain areas. No one is knowledgeable or efficient in every area of life. While one person may know many things pertaining to a specific subject, they may be totally lacking in knowledge about many more subject areas. So knowledge alone certainly cannot define a person. You are made of many elements. To adequately define yourself you must look into every aspect of the traits, qualities and properties that you possess. You are heart, spirit, soul, mind, and body. You are also the sum total of all your life experiences. You were created in the image of God with the potential to inherit many wonderful benefits. Your personality, and characteristic traits, may define you today, however, you should be forever growing, changing, and maturing. You are a mortal human being with fears and anxieties, cares and concerns, and imperfections that all growing human beings possess. Many of your fears and anxieties, and some of your cares and concerns, may be unwarranted but they are an intricate part of you until *YOU* decide to confess them, along with everything that you discover within your self.

Do not just acknowledge the flaws, but make mental notes of the good traits as well. Experience the freedom of saying, "I have fears and anxieties about my career choices or my love life," or whatever you are afraid or anxious about. Once you have made the initial decision to make them known to yourself, you can make the decision to dig them up by the roots and cast them as far away from you as possible. But be sure to replace them very quickly with such things as courage, boldness, assurance, peace and tranquillity. You are like many other human beings in many, many ways. You may have defined yourself by your ability or your inability to succeed in some area or another.

Remember success is a rather personal, relative term. Some people believe that they have reached the pinnacle of success when they have acquired a myriad of material possessions. Others may declare themselves successful when they have reached certain goals, educational or professional, that they have been striving towards. You can set the standards for your own high points in life. When you know who you are and have a good idea of where you want to go, and are actively traveling in that direction without regard to what others are doing, you may have reached a greater pinnacle of success than you ever thought possible. Success is reached when you have made private, personal decisions about your life and they have been good profitable decisions. Success may come when you have gained something that you planned for, something that you wanted to acquire, or have attempted to do or achieved some goals that you have set. You can be successful at many things. Some of your most successful moments may come after some of your failures and the lessons you learned from those failures. Success does not define you. You must define success for yourself. It is not success in things associated with the material world that will bring peace to the mind, love to the heart, rest for the soul and gladness to the spirit. It is fulfillment of your purpose in life that brings that kind of success. If you are in harmony with your inner person, you are successful! When you know exactly what you want it is always easier to plan for it and put forth your best effort towards achieving it. Do not be quickly deceived. Many financially successful people would give almost anything to have peace of mind.

No one can ever tell you who you are. It is up to you to tell yourself who you are, not who people think you are, or who you wish you were, but the real person who lives inside of the body you wear. Only you can make the discovery. By knowing that a great portion of your life equals to the sum total of all of your experiences, you should be encouraged to examine your all experiences more closely. Remember, most of your experiences good, bad or otherwise, are the end results of decisions you have made or decisions that you failed to make (which amounts to decisions by omission). There may be a few decisions that shape portions of your life that were made for you, but there comes a time in everyone's life when they can do something about their situation. If this new relationship that you are entering into with yourself is to be productive, you must not allow yourself to wallow in any distasteful state that you find yourself in. You can make the necessary adjustments to change your mind set, your spiritual state, and even transform your heart to become the person that God created you to be. Transformation is within your reach. When you believe that you are uniquely special and make a decision to fall in love with yourself, you may be able to define yourself as the wonderful person who is a work in progress. *Living life to the full* means to be the very best that you can be every day. You may have inherited your nature from the first family but you do not have to let it influence you anymore. You were created in the image of God with the ability to acquire a divine nature that will correspond to His nature. All this may seem impossible to you now but, if you are already a member of the royal family of God you know

32

that, *With God all things are possible.*

It probably took many experiences and much time to make you into the person that you really found within. You may not like all that you found within yourself on your self-discovery journey. It may take a while to break old habits and form a new mold if you decide to make some adjustments to the person that you discovered. As long as you remember that, *all things are possible for those who believe,* you will be able to make all the necessary adjustments at the appropriate time.

Hopefully, you have an idea of who you are, and many of the things that went into the making of the special person that you are. Even though you may not feel special, you have a wonderful opportunity to become special to yourself. Use all of your resources to their best advantage, and begin to renew your mind. Do not quit until you believe that you are special to God and to yourself. Once you believe that you are special you will expect to be treated like someone special in your future relationships.

Upon exiting from your tour, I have a few suggestions to make that could be important for your future growth. I have provided an example for you to write down all the positive virtues that you discovered about yourself. You should make a decision to embrace and nurture each one of your positive virtures individually. When you feel like berating yourself for some of your less profitable decisions, review your positive virtues. You might decide that you are worthy of the person God created you to be after all. In a separate column write down all the qualities that you perceived as negative during your self-discovery journey. Examine each one of the qualities thoroughly. Once you are certain of how you want to handle each quality, make definite decisions and plans to deal with each one, beginning with the ones you believe are the most repulsive. Plan to discipline yourself to become all that you can be. Review each list on a regular basis. Mark a line through each negative quality that you overcame by digging it up and getting rid of it. Write down what you replaced it with at the bottom of your positive list. Remember, it is very important for you to take responsibility for everything, good or bad that were consequences of your decisions. Even the qualities that you find distasteful that did not result from your decisions can be changed. Do not waste precious time blaming someone else for habits, traits and other unsatisfactory qualities that you discovered.

Make a decision to establish wholesome, productive relationships that enhance your life in some way. Look in the mirror every morning and every night, and tell your reflection what you think of the person you see. Tell that reflection why you feel the way you do. Discipline yourself to stick to your plan. Your goal should be to someday look at that reflection and honestly say, "I am very proud of who you have become and I love you just the way you are, however; I realize that you are still a work in progress." When you can truly say that you have come to terms with the person God created you to be, you are in the process of falling in love with yourself, and entering into a wonderful, rewarding relationship. If that feeling of exhilaration that you hoped for does not come for many months, or even many years, do not give up hope. Keep working towards reaching your personal pinnacle of success. God is not through with you yet. You will always be a work in progress as long as you are growing up and not down, and developing into a better person than you were yesterday. You can take the self-discovery tour as often as you feel the need to do so. It may be a good idea to re-assess yourself frequently to make sure nothing negative slipped within while you were not looking. This might be a good time to begin a self-discovery journal. It is always encouraging to look back over your life and see how you have grown. It is also encouraging for everyone to come face-to-face with the person they really are and with what they really have to work. This self-discovery tour will probably reveal many good, admirable qualities.

Positive Qualities

Patience: Ability to wait on whatever I hope for without growing impatient or weary.

Decision: Continue to practice patience in every area of my life.

Plan: If I find myself becoming anxious or frustrated, I will stop whatever I am doing and write down my reasons for being anxious or frustrated and examine each one. I will then decide to pray for guidance or direction in accordance with Proverbs 3:5-6, *Trust in the Lord with all your heart and lean not on your own understanding; in all your ways acknowledge Him, and He will make your paths straight.*

Discipline: Continue to acknowledge the presence of the Lord until anxiety/frustration passes. Call a trusted friend to discuss anxieties. Seek spiritual/professional help if there is a prolongation of any of these feelings.

Negative Qualities

Fears: I am afraid that I can never measure up to my parents expectations. I am afraid of what the future holds for me because I have no knowledge of my entire heritage. I am afraid of failures. I am afraid of many things that I have not yet identified.

Reasons: I am not sure about all of my fears yet. I have never met my father and I am afraid of what I may have inherited from him. I really want to meet him, but I am afraid of rejection.

Plan: I will list all my fears and examine each one individually.

Decision: I will acknowledge my fears and not try to hide them anymore. I will be honest with myself about each fear and put forth my best effort to eliminate them one at a time. I will make a definite decision to look for my father whenever I overcome my fear of rejection or when I think I am ready to face the possibility of rejection.

Discipline: I will make sure I face at least one fear each day and seek help if it becomes necessary as I try to find ways to eliminate them. Facing my fears will become a part of my daily meditations and devotions.

These are only examples of how one can begin to handle the elements that they discovered. Each person must choose the path that he/she will follow to discover, identify and re-create the person that he/she discovered.

Learning about one's self is only one phase of learning about wholesome, healthy, balanced relationships. There are still many things about other people, who enter into relationships, that one should know before making a decision to entrust some of their precious qualities into the care of anyone.

Chapter Two

WHAT IS THERE TO KNOW?

Do your future and all to which you can relate

seem to hang in the balance, yet you don't want to wait

until you have enough widson and knowledge to know

that being in a hurry is not the right way to go?

What is so hard about getting together with other people and sharing your life experiences, your emotional and intellectual qualities, and maybe a few resources? People are basically the same. After all, everyone seems to be pursuing similar dreams. Everyone wants peace, love, acceptance, and happiness. Meeting people who have been trampled under the feet of life, and establishing a relationship with them, should be no problem. All it takes is a little understanding, a little help, and a little love to help them get their lives together. They will repay you with gratitude and probably an everlasting friendship. It does not matter what type of relationship someone intends to establish, it really should not be hard. There is really not that much to know. Business partners, looking for someone to share their dreams and lend a little assistance, just need someone to believe in them and help them to fulfill their dreams. What is all the delaying, waiting and fuss about? If people are loved enough, encouraged enough, and trusted enough, any type of relationship can work! Those are the sentiments of many people who have entered into relationships with unrealistic expectations. Some people who believe that relationships are no big thing, and there is really nothing to know, are disappointed by people who do not live up to their expectations. Some of those responses may have some validity. Basically, most people are similar in many ways but each person is different in many more ways. Love and understanding cannot enable some people to overcome their shortcomings. Some people never "get it together" no matter how much love, understanding and time they have. Everyone is looking for something or someone that can bring peace to their heart, quiet their spirit and satisfaction their soul. People seek out others to enter into relationships with because they want to feel secure and be a part of something living and growing all the time. Inner peace comes to many people when they have the assurance that someone somewhere loves them and accepts them just like they are. Those who have never experienced unconditional love and acceptance have built-in places within that long for those things. Not knowing where to look, or how to recognize the things they long for, can create many problems. Those people pacify themselves with the belief that there is no such thing as unconditional love and acceptance. Just because they impose conditions on their love and acceptance of others they are comfortable in their belief that this is what everyone does. However, relationships are not exactly about changing other people's beliefs and ideals, and they are not all about making other people feel good about themselves. Most relationships are about being in the company of others on whom one can depend. They are also about sharing the joys and sorrows of others. Everyone is inclined to associate with others who share interests, activities and purposes similar to theirs. How can anyone know what the interests and purposes of others are without getting to know something about them? How can a person know what his/her interests are unless they can honestly define themselves and know what they expect of others and what they have to share in a relationship?

People's needs are as numerous and diverse as people are. Attempting to share in interests, meet needs, understand goals and aspirations, and feel productive and comfortable in a relationship, is not always as simple as getting together to share a few laughs. There is a vast difference between entering into a productive relationship and being acquainted with someone. While one may be aware of a person and get to know some surface things about him/her, that type of association is much less intimate than a close friendship or any type of interpersonal relationship. Acquaintances may share a few things about their interests and purposes until they decide to become more familiar. Most relationships begin with becoming acquainted with each other; however, it is the acquisition of knowledge about others that determines if there are any common threads that can connect them in a closer relationship. All relationships are not equal and were not intended to be equal. There are some specific relationships that are designed to serve specific purposes. People should be complementary to each other or at least compatible with each other so that they can comfortably enjoy the fruits of a healthy relationship. Each person should learn how to define their relationships according to their own priorities. Sometimes family connections are more important than casual friendships and relationships between spouses usually have a much higher priority than parental family connections. It is important to know what a healthy, productive relationship entails before becoming totally involved in any close, binding types of relationships.

Most people choose to enter into a relationship with social friends, business associates and partners for life. Getting to know the person one plans to interact with on a regular basis beforehand may prevent some pain, disappointments and frustrations later on. People should know what they expect to give of themselves and what they expect others to share in the same relationship. Entering into a relationship with the thought of "letting the chips fall where they may," is like aiming at nothing and willingly accepting whatever comes one's way. When your aim is specific, you will not be inclined to accept a reasonable facsimile of what you want or expect. If you are a reasonable, emotionally healthy person, you will most likely wait for the real thing to enter into your life. However, when you are not aiming at anything in particular you become easy prey for a relationship that may not meet your needs. Some people are "lucky" enough to reach a mutual agreement with someone that just happened to come into their lives. Some of the things people share in some relationships are too valuable to be left entirely to chance. Many, many "chance" relationships do not work out. People who enter into relationships blindly often become emotionally, spiritually, financially or physically injured when they are committed to such relationships.

Knowledge is empowering when it is rightly applied. If you want to become powerful and be in control of some of your life experiences, you should acquire all the knowledge you can about the day-to-day operations of relationships. Learn what a relationship is. Delve into the inner workings of what makes a relationship reasonable and healthy. Get a practical understanding of each new acquaintance before you decide that you have a common thread that can possibly connect you. Make sure you know what type of relationship the other person want, before you enter into a new relationship. In some types of relationships, it may not be easy or possible to change the terms of your pledge once the relationship is underway. Do not be in a desperate hurry to force yourself into a relationship that does not seem to fit your purpose and expectations. Remind yourself that you have time, because your future may hang in the balance and you may waste more time than you think you are saving when you make hasty decisions. Know that if you force yourself into a relationship that does not fit, or settle for what seems to be available right now because you think you may be missing a golden opportunity, you are selling yourself short. You may be reserving a space within yourself for future failure and disappointment.

A reasonable, healthy relationship, planted firmly in the soil of common sense, is an association between two or more reasonable people who already have some similar interests, activities and purposes. The reason most people enter into relationship with each other is to share the things they already have in common. People with similar interests, activities and purposes often have a mental connection that can bind them closer together. When they come together for the first time they seem to be drawn to each other by an invisible, yet common, thread. This mental connection can exist between casual friends, close friends, family members and potential partners for life. After exchanging ideas, thoughts and messages for a few minutes the mental connection between them is usually unveiled through the sharing of logical, common sense values. They feel comfortable enough to ask and answer questions that will help define the type of relationship they plan to enter into. Sometimes they ponder over each other's answers and comments before they decide that the elements necessary to establish a relationship are evident. Sometimes the connection is spiritual as well as mental. People who are contented with who they are do not usually feel pressured to make hasty decisions about establishing relationships right away, even with others whose interests, purposes and mental/spiritual connections are similar to their own. It may take quite a few encounters before communication flows easily and is relaxed.

Communication on the same level, in the same language among associates is one of the elements of a reasonable, healthy relationship. The exchange of ideas, thoughts and messages can usually be assessed on the first or second encounter between people. Reasonable people employ all their senses in getting to know others before they decide that they want to share portions of their lives with them. Mutual sharing in the cares and concerns of others is one of the things that makes relationships worth while. Mutual sharing means both parties agree on the type of relationship they have with each other. Each person within the same relationship is concerned about, and participates equally or jointly in the responsibilities, interests and agreed-upon properties. This often comes naturally with people who have mental and/or spiritual connections and share similar purposes. The types of property people share will depend on the type of relationship they have. Properties can be tangible or intangible.

People rarely think about what they are in the process of making a special effort to share when they enter into a relationship with someone else. Interests, activities and purpose include almost every tangible and intangible asset that is valuable to people. Emotions and intellectual abilities, things that a person is concerned about, dreams and aspirations, all come under the heading of interests, activities and purposes. What one anticipates sharing will depend upon the type of relationship he/she enters into. When a reasonable person think about what he/she intends to share, they should want to make sure they know about the principles, moral character and intellectual capabilities of the others with whom they are about to enter into an agreement. They must also consider the benefits and advantages, as well as the lack of benefits and the disadvantages, of entering into a specific type of relationship. Time, energy and possibly financial resources cannot be excluded from the thought process beforehand. In close relationships with friends or potential partners for life, you are actually consenting to share your activities and just about everything you do with someone that you are not grossly familiar with, unless you take the time to know all that you can know about them.

The time for self-indulgence becomes a thing of the past. You may be agreeing to share your space and habits with someone. You may have different ways of doing things or different ideas about your participation in certain activities. It is important to get a practical understanding of other people's abilities to perform within the boundaries of reason. When differences arise, if logical conclusions are to be reached, everyone must be capable of making just and right judgments within the boundaries of common sense or reason. Some of the things that you may be called upon to participate in may stretch or bend some of your ideas, plans, and thought processes totally out of shape. You should be able to recover without resentment or other residual effects if the relationship is to remain intact and continue to grow. Sometimes you may be the one to bend or stretch the ideas, thoughts or plans of others for the good or growth and development of the relationship. You should feel confident that the relationship is healthy enough to withstand the pressure without affecting its integrity. People should be ready for some give and take when they enter into relationships. People will be coming from different backgrounds, forming common bonds. It usually takes time for all the necessary adjustments to be made before a relationship "jells." Different people will probably have different feelings about taking portions of something that belongs to them and distributing it among others. What one proposes to share is not always one of the major issues that can cause problems. Sometimes the idea of sharing may present major problems for some people. Even people who seem to have mental and spiritual connections, and are interested in many of the same things, are still individuals. They bring whatever personalities and traits that they have into each relationship. Selfish people remain selfish until they have a desire to change. Many people believe that they are okay in whatever state they find themselves. There will probably be differences of opinions about many things. Differences in the methods of doing certain things, and many other differences, may come up in close relationships. Basic principles and other characteristic traits become involved in the establishing of healthy relationships, especially in the way people choose to settle disagreements.

There is really a lot to know that could be very helpful to reasonable people who want to enter into healthy relationships that will last. The closer people become as friends in any type of relationship, the more important it becomes for them to agree upon similar principles. Basic truths, rules and standards that determine the morals and ethics that govern the way people act makes a big difference in how they relate to each other in a relationship. People in close relationships should agree upon the essential elements or qualities that define just and right behavior. Many of the laws that determine how human beings should relate to each other were extracted from the Ten Commandments in the Bible. *You shall not murder. You shall not commit adultery. You shall not steal. You shall not give false testimony against your neighbor* (Ex. 20: 13-16) are among the laws that are still the foundation for acceptable behavioral standards. These laws are still in effect today. Some people behave according to the principle set forth in the *Golden Rule, Do to others as you would have them do to you* (Lk. 6:31). It does not matter whether one set of rules is right or wrong, or good or bad, people are very particular about their own principles. People usually behave in accordance with what they *believe* to be right and just in accordance with their personal impressions.

Principles involve initial socialization processes and how people were trained. Belief systems may be at the very core of many people's identity. What and in whom a person believes involves the inner workings of a person's heart, soul, and spirit. If drastic differences of opinion arise involving an individual's principles, each person may be put in a position to make a decision about the relationship or their principles. If one's principles must be compromised to maintain harmony in the relationship, the most important issue will prevail. However, there will always be a "bone of contention" over that issue if one person has to feel pressured to compromise his/her principles. Belief systems, purposes, aspirations and specific goals in life are all related to the mental and spiritual life of a person. A person's belief system may take on a sacred interpretation. It does not matter what or whom they choose to worship. Therefore, this issue cannot be over-looked or taken lightly. It should be one of the major areas for discussion, and an agreement should be reached among people who are about to enter into a close relationship with each other. Conflict over religious matters can arise among close friends, family members and partners for life. Some people believe that God is the only true and living God. They have total confidence in His existence and abilities to be omnipresent, omnipotent and omniscient. Because of their personal experiences and faith in God, along with any transformation that may have taken place within their hearts, souls, and spirits when they entered into a relationship with Him, He is the only real God to them. Some people believe in different gods who are specific in their duties. These gods may have a full range of attributes that seem to inspire people to pay tribute to them. Those who believe in different gods have confidence in the principles of their religious beliefs also. When dissimilarities are apparent in this area, one of three things will usually happen: Those who are not very firm in their beliefs and are not convicted by the principles of their religion may make a concession in the name of peace. Others may agree to disagree if there can be no simple resolution or combination of belief systems without producing emotionally or spiritually harmful effects. Some people make a decision not to enter a relationship or to exit an already existing one if they cannot agree on religious matters. However, when there is a compromise of any sort and everyone decides to remain in the relationship, the depth of the relationship can be negatively affected.

People who believe in God, and have absolute confidence in Biblical principles, also believe that regular, close relationships with people who habitually attack their belief system can depreciate their fellowship with Christ. Trying to maintain a relationship where basic principles are opposed is also a source of undue stress on everyone. When a believer become bonded in a vice-like connection with non-believers, the believer's fellowship with Christ can be interrupted if he/she permits the relationship to continue. Believers are advised against such bonds. *Do not be yoked together with unbelievers* (2 Cor. 6:14). Application to that Scripture is often made in reference to bonding in marriage; however, when rightly applied it also means forming a partnership with anyone who has enough influence over your interests, activities and purposes to disrupt your fellowship with Christ.

Everyone should know in whom and what they believe, to be certain of what they will be willing to give up, take on or concede to. The decision to yield or not to yield to someone else's belief system should be clarified before entering into a close, personal relationship. Purpose and belief systems may share equal importance but are not always connected. Sometimes principles and belief systems are affected by an individual's purpose. People who share common purposes are agreeing to share some of the important things they intend to focus their attention, thoughts, feelings and efforts on. One's purpose should be clearly defined beforehand. Purposes usually involves some of the goals people set for themselves based on a tangible or material concept. Some relationships can enhance the goals of others and some relationships may lack the necessary qualities to support one or more persons' goals. It is very important that everyone understands the reason for each relationship they enter into. The terms or conditions of the relationship should be clearly defined. They must also decide if the relationship is more important than their personal goals and objectives. Each person should ask themselves how each relationship will affect their goals and how they will feel about the people involved if they abandon or delay their own goals. Roots of bitterness can begin to develop when one or more persons' goals are delayed, abandoned or never come to pass because of the demands of the relationship.

The reason some relationships exist is to get together, have fun, play cards or other games, discuss things peculiar to certain groups of people, etc. Other types of relationships exist to support people with similar concerns in one or two specific areas. Some people enter into relationships with others for the sole purpose of deceiving them for personal gain. When people understand their own reason for entering relationships, it is easier for them to know when their needs are not being met or their purpose is different. These are also some of the reasons that it makes good, common sense to get to know people before agreeing to share some of your precious assets with them. Be as concerned about the good character of others as you are about your own reputation and virtues. People who practice to deceive do so intentionally and can usually justify their behavior. Never, never believe that you can love or trust anyone enough to change their character. Most people are very comfortable with themselves. Even people with some disastrous character flaws believe that they are basically good. You can only change your own character. Others change only if or when they feel a need to change. Keep in mind that some people hate changes. Changes are not easy to make for most people. Making character changes involves making a decision, adopting different mind sets, and disciplining one's self to abandon old habits and replace them with something better. The need and decision to change arise from inside of a person. Entering into a relationship with the idea of changing someone can predispose a person to disappointment and frustration.

You probably know by now that people are the sum total of their emotional responses, impressions, learned and environmental influences, along with their personal life experiences and belief systems. The quality of a person's character is revealed in the way they behave and interact with others. When people make a decision to wait until they have enough knowledge about others before entering into a close, personal relationship, they are saving themselves from what may be future disaster. When people spend enough time in the presence of their associates, they are privileged to view more important aspects of their impressions, responses, beliefs and life experiences. You can learn a lot about people by making use of the data you receive during general conversation when no one is trying to impress anyone. Make use of this information in determining the quality of a person's character. Pay strict attention to what others have to say about those that you intend to enter into a relationship with. Observe temperaments, moods, inclinations, responses and logical deductions made by anyone you intend to enter into a close relationship with. Learn the elements of a healthy, reasonable relationship and compare them to the character of those with whom you intend to share portions of your life. This scrutiny should include friends, some family members with whom there is little close contact, and, most importantly, potential partners for life.

Some of the elements of a healthy, reasonable relationship include trust, loyalty, honesty, respect, commitment, and effective communication. You should explore each element so that you know what is expected of you and what you should expect of others. Make sure you measure up before you set high standards for others. It would be unfair to expect more of others than you are willing to give. Remember, there is going to be a mutual exchange of emotional and intellectual qualities along with many other valuable assets. Just as you expect others to be particular about the handling of your "fragile properties," others are equally concerned about how you handle their "fragile property." Keep in mind, relationships should enhance existing lifestyles instead of imposing stress and other burdens. Everyone who displays good characteristic traits in certain settings are not always who people think they are. Think of how you behave in different situations. That is why it is a good idea to observe people under some extreme conditions before concluding that their character is above reproach. It is easy for anyone to learn protocol for specific events and follow that protocol. People who know the principles of good behavior according to the accepted standards usually put forth every effort to live by those principles even when they think no one is watching them. The best time to get to know something about the quality of one's character is when they are not "performing." People with good moral character, whose intentions are honorable, do not have to be pressured into doing right. When you place total confidence in someone else, your trust is in their abilities to perform according to standards as well as the integrity of their character. Trust demands the releasing of both, emotional and intellectual qualities into the care of the one(s) in whom trust is placed. Assurance of each person's good intentions should be validated beforehand. Everyone involved in the same relationship should be able to depend on each other to behave in a reasonable, right and just manner. Making sure associates are dependable should be verified before entrusting precious, valued assets into their care. It is important for each person to be willing and capable of conforming to reason, justice and truth, and to behave in an appropriate manner before the relationship can be beneficial for everyone.

Trust is closely associated with honesty and loyalty. They all incorporate faithfulness, sincerity and unquestionable beliefs in the character of a person. People can only be honest about things they know or believe to be true. Sometimes people deviate from accepted truths because they believe their versions of reality are true. However, people who deliberately avoid telling the truth intend to deceive. Many seemingly good, intelligent people who display impeccable mannerisms convey false impressions intentionally. As much as you may want to trust some people, it is wise to beware of people who set out to deceive you. Deceptive people are not trustworthy, honest and loyal by nature. It takes practice to become habitually deceptive and dishonest! These traits are usually intricate parts of the character of people who intend to deceive. Although you cannot change their character, they may be capable of disrupting your life in more ways than you can imagine, especially if you trust them with valuable assets. If you observe people closley enough, you should be able to single out people who exhibit the following deceptive traits. People who talk fast before hearing anything you have to say usually have conversations that are confusing and convoluted. When questioned about some of these confusing issues, they may tell you that you must have misunderstood what they said. They seem to have pre-arranged answers to most questions. Maybe they have been questioned about their behavior before. Deceptive people can usually justify everything they say or do. They never take responsibility for their negative behavior. They habitually blame someone else for their failures and poor decisions. They are known to raise questions about absolute and relative truth. Those who deliberately deceive have no respect for the interests, possessions or feelings of others. They are usually absorbed in themselves and their personal interest. This prevents them from being loyal to anyone else. When people have a devoted attachment and true affection for others, they are genuinely concerned about others' emotions and their properties.

Being in accord regarding respect is vital to the health of a relationship. People who honor others and deem them worthy of appreciation, courtesy and consideration put forth every effort to avoid violating them in any way. When people respect each other, they regard others and all they stand for, very highly. When respect is mutual, each person shares responsibility for protecting the reputation, character and possessions of the other. There is no exploitation for personal gain. If judgment errors are made and illogical conclusions are reached by others in a relationship, respectable people feel the sorrow they generously express to each other. A reasonable explanation is usually forthcoming to prevent a breakdown in the relationship. Most communication is usually apologetic and frequent, to make sure everyone understands the intent of the heart.

Any relationship that grows beyond the initial getting-acquainted stage must have effective communication between the participants. For communication to be effective, thoughts, ideas and messages must be conveyed in language that is easily understood by everyone. Mental and spiritual connections between people do not include mind reading abilities. Verbal expression is often necessary to get a point across. When some people attempt to impress others by using words that may be hard to understand, and the question,"What did you mean?" or "What did you say?" is asked frequently, communication is ineffective. Productive communication can create an atmosphere of freedom where conversation flows comfortably among people. Everyone understands the other in their own language! There is a feeling of relaxation that is inviting to anyone wishing to express themselves. Nonproductive communication can be compared to attempts to listen to a radio that is not clearly on any station. Static overshadows most of the messages, and there seems to be a shift between two stations. Partial statements from each station may come in clearly from both stations every now and then. It is next to impossible to make sense of the message from either station. Long episodes of silence in a conversation can put a strain on attempts to communicate with others. I will share an incident about communication that had the potential to discourage me from entering into a specific type of relationship.

During a period of time in my life, I had undergone a transformation. I was single, with a few friends, some colleagues and professional peers, and a few church members with whom I interacted away from church on occasion. With each group of people there were specific topics we talked about. However, when ever I dated, after the initial getting-acquainted questions and answers, there were long breaks in the flow of conversation. Seemingly, I was always trying to think of something to say. During those times I wondered what people found to talk about and laugh about who were with each other day-in and day-out. Ineffective communication is not just boring; it can be burdensome as well. I just did not want to be bothered with the discomfort anymore. Years went by and then I met someone with whom I connected mentally and shared many interests. Conversing was natural and easy. Once we were able to communicate with each other on the same "frequency," without all the unnecessary static, we could honestly compare interests and purposes. We had an opportunity to assess each other's emotional and intellectual qualities and put our moral integrity to the test. We openly discussed intentions and plans for reaching our goals. After a few conversations, it was clear that we were in accord with each other, and, although there were some differences, we respected each other mutually. As time went by and communication continued to be open and honest, we learned enough about each other to place our valuable assets into each other's care. We were able to acquire enough knowledge to gain a practical understanding of each other through effective communication. Our theories of who we represented were based on our behavior which proved to be consistent with our theories. We dreamed a lot but we were real about speculations and dreams and actual achievable goals. Each of us were capable of delivering everything that we promised each other. Before we made a commitment of any kind, we were both convinced that we were about to enter into a relationship that was purposeful and beneficial to both of us. Now we spend hours laughing, talking, planning and exchanging ideas. Sometimes after spending all day together, we talk throughout the night. Effective communication is at the heart and soul of all wholesome relationships. Sometimes there will be disagreements, and all effective communication may not be pleasant, but exchanging ideas, sharing thoughts and verbal expressions of feelings is one way of exposing the real you to other people.

Many people may have honorable intentions but fail to communicate them to others, which can (and often do) lead to wrong assumptions. Many relationships are all about getting up close and personal with each other. Effective communication is the hallmark for any type of relationship Communication is one way of permitting people to get a good, basic understanding of all the things they are expected to share in a relationship. Make sure you can communicate in a way that is comfortable and lends itself to freedom of expression before making a commitment.

A commitment should be the last element that people "activate" in establishing a relationship. A commitment is a written, assumed, or verbally expressed agreement between two or more people, enforceable by law in some instances. The type of commitment one makes depends upon the type of relationship they are entering into. A commitment represents an earnest pledge to be emotionally bound to the ideas of others, and to perform certain duties and tasks in a certain way. It is a promise or declaration that you will or will not do some specific things. Most people who are concerned with the principles of right and wrong show deep sincerity in attempting to live up to their promises. When my husband, Larry, and I made the decision to become friends, we verbally agreed to the standards that would govern our relationship. Once we agreed upon the rules that we would be guided by, we made an informal pledge within our hearts. The pledge we made to each other was very serious. Even pledging to be guided by certain standards is serious enough to warrant quality time and effort. Sometimes disagreements in this area can make a difference in the decision to abandon the idea of a relationship, or to continue with plans to establish one. Things do not get better after the commitment is made. Rarely does a person change his/her mind about principles and standards. If the differences of opinion threatens to be disruptive later on, it may be wise to wait before making a commitment, especially if you are contemplating a lifetime partnership. Once you become emotionally and spiritually bound to someone, it may not be feasible to re-negotiate the terms of the agreement.

People should establish relationships for the joy of sharing portions of their lives with someone else. However, there should be some boundaries, guidelines and terms that keep the relationship within the defined boundaries. When people know what to expect and know what is expected of them, it makes life much easier. It eliminates the need of having to figure out what to do. Lack of understanding, unrealistic expectations, and unmet needs are major reasons for failures in relationships. Most of these deficiencies are due to lack of effective communication. Some people believe that they are failures because they did not know what was expected of them or what it took to meet the needs of others. When the elements of a healthy relationship are put into practice, it is possible for people to achieve their real goals.

Generally, people are looking for someone to make them happy, love them and accept them unconditionally. They may believe that if they could find someone to give them these things, they could achieve peace within their innermost beings. All of that may be too much to ask of someone else. People cannot give or share anything that they do not possess. They usually have a problem giving or receiving things that they cannot identify. Most of the things that many, many human beings seek from others can only be found within themselves. Love is defined in many ways. It is said to be an intense attraction for another person based on personal ties. It is also defined as a deep tenderness and concern felt for another person. It is expressed as God's mercy and benevolence towards humans, and humankinds' devotion and adoration of God. Love is expressed as a feeling of kindness and brother-hood towards others. It is often viewed as just a feeling; or an emotional response, or something that is born within the heart. It is impossible for anyone else but God, through the Holy

Spirit, to bring forth the birth of unconditional love within the heart of someone else!

This does not mean that people cannot love each other in the ways they know how to give and receive love. They can express what they view as love in ways that are familiar to them. However, they must be in possession of love before they can share it. Good will and emotional feelings produce actions consistent with those feelings. Divine love is capable of producing a change in a person's attitude and perceptions. Love, as the world perceives it, is often transient and is only expressed under favorable conditions. God's love is the only love that is eternal and unconditional. His Love is comes with peace.

Peace which is the absence of strife, turmoil and disturbances within the mind, heart, soul, and spirit, is also born within. The outward expressions of tranquillity and harmony can only be shared with others who are sensitive to peaceful expressions. Of course the opposite of love is animosity and the opposite of peace is turmoil. People who suffer from inner turmoil and animosity usually want to rid themselves of those negative feelings but do not know how. All these negative expressions can be like heavy, burdens that people carry with them wherever they go. They are usually looking for some place to unload their burdens. Even if people dump these qualities on someone else, it does not give them the freedom they desire. These are among the qualities that anyone who takes the self-discovery trip should consciously discard and replace with positive qualities. Disappointment is usually added to all other negative feelings when unrealistic expectations are not met. The carriers of these negative qualities are usually very uncomfortable or even in pain. However, they do not always see themselves as the problem. They tend to blame someone else for their inability to make them happy, give them love and accept them, or bring them into a state of peace and harmony. There is not much joy within a person carrying all that baggage. Please understand that you <u>cannot</u> fix them and make their problems go away. All you can do is attempt to encourage them to seek assistance. They may be suffering emotionally or spiritually. Whatever peace, love and happiness emotionally or spiritually injured people find is usually temporary. Rarely, if ever, will there be any real joy within their hearts.

People can share in each other's happiness, but happiness cannot be passed around from one person to another. It cannot be captured and retained for future use. It comes and goes with the occurrence of delightful or pleasant events. People interested in establishing and maintaining healthy relationships want to share joys, sorrows, disappointments and life experiences with others. There is a difference between joy and happiness. Joy is a gladness divinely transplanted within the heart that remains there in spite of unhappy situations or circumstances. The joy is in the Lord. People who possess this joy are as interested in giving of themselves and their assets as they are in receiving the benefits that reasonable, healthy relationships can offer.

There will always be people looking for someone to share the experiences of life with. Waiting for specific people who can fulfill your specific needs can save you a lot of time and disappointment. Relationships are necessary to the well-being of all human beings. To make them as pleasant as possible, people should know how to differentiate between true fulfillment and immediate gratification. Fulfillment is really what most people are seeking anyway. People were born with certain needs. When those needs are not met, there are empty places or voids within that seem to gnaw like a sore that will not heal or an itch that cannot be scratched. Other people have intense desires that give them the same feelings. These needs and desires are specific. Some can be fulfilled by specific relationships and others are filled when the specific desires come to pass. People are not always sure of what it would take to fill each empty place within themselves or how to get what they desire. They only know that they want or need something to relieve the unpleasant sensations or feelings of emptiness. Some people try to fill the empty places with food, others may engage in numerous sexual encounters or non-specific relationships that may gratify them temporarily. Temporary gratification can bring pleasure immediately after receiving whatever it was that the person sought; however, the pleasurable sensation does not bring the need or desire to an end. Unless the specific need or desire is met, the unpleasant sensation will return continuously. The unpleasant sensations of unfulfillment can be likened to a longing for a specific type of food. A person can eat many things in an attempt to satisfy that specific longing, to no avail. The longing does not go away until the specific item has been acquired and consumed. Fulfillment makes the gnawing go away and fills the empty place within. There may be numerous empty places that are "reserved" for something or someone specific within every individual.

People define these empty places within in many different ways. Dana told me her story about a longing she had within herself for years and how she found fulfillment. She described the longing as a dark hole or a void deep within herself that she could not quite identify, but she felt the effects of the emptiness constantly. She knew that she needed something to fill in that hole. This is her story.

For as long as Dana could remember she had shared her home with her mother Edith, her grandmother Allison, and her younger siblings. She could not remember receiving any affection or attention from Edith. Her grandmother always took care of her and made sure her needs were met. Dana said she longed for a relationship with her mother. She tried everything possible to win Edith's affections but Edith was indifferent to her. Dana was sure that the unpleasant sensation within her would cease to be if only she could be loved by her mother. That never happened during her childhood and throughout most of her young adulthood.

Edith was not unkind to Dana and she did not mistreat her; she just failed to nurture her the way Dana longed to be nurtured. Dana said she resented her mother for her indifference. Years went by and Dana began her own life away from Edith and Allison. She was introduced to the Christian concept by some of her friends. She went to church with them and began to learn some interesting things about Jesus Christ. One day she made the decision to enter into a relationship with God through Jesus Christ. Dana said that she was not quite sure when the unpleasant sensation within her left. One day, following her initial acceptance of the gift of God's love, she noticed that the dark hole within her had been filled with light and she no longer felt that empty feeling inside. Dana thought that that place could only be filled by her mother's love and attention. When that specific need was met, Dana was able to forgive Edith and enter into a healthy relationship with her based on love. Dana could share the love she had acquired with her mother. They have a wonderful parent-child relationship that is not overshadowed by past experiences.

When people really know what they want or need, it makes fulfillment of that need much easier. It prevents people from entering and exiting non-specific relationships that may be doomed before they are established. Some people believe that their inner longings are for job satisfaction. They may strive to climb the corporate ladder and succeed in reaching the top, only to find out that the places within themselves are still empty. They may strive to gain material possessions, but become disgruntled when they realize that there is no joy in ownership unless there is someone specific to share their possessions with. Many wealthy people marry and divorce constantly. They may be seeking fulfillment but settling for immediate gratification. Perhaps they think that sooner or later they will "get it right." It may never occur to them that a marital relationship may not be the thing that can bring their inner longing to an end. Joy, peace, and the things that make life worth living may seem like unattainable illusions to many people. Some people who seem to possess a few worldly or material possessions are often more content within themselves than some of the wealthiest people around. When most people's needs are met, and they have reached total fulfillment in most of the areas of their lives, they have joy within their hearts that cannot be taken away. It is a real blessing to identify with the writer in Philippians who says, *I have learned the secret of being content in nay and every situation, whether well fed or hungry, whether living in plenty or in want (4:12).* Material things can make life more comfortable externally but they do very little to bring inner longings to a close. When fulfillment for a specific need comes, it brings that specific need to an end forever. One will never long for that specific desire to be fulfilled again. My dear friend, Lisa Artis knew exactly what she desired and she knew that once her desire was fulfilled, her longing would come to an end. Lisa allowed me to share her story with you.

Lisa said she always dreamed of having two children, a boy and a girl. She said that her heart ached and she felt an emptiness deep within her innermost being that she knew could only be filled by having two children of her own. Lisa loved the Lord and took Him at His word when He said, *ask and it will be given to you*(Luke 11:9). She asked and asked all her Christian friends to pray that God would give her some babies. Years went by and she did not conceive but she never gave up hope and never ceased to pray. One of her friends asked her if she had considered adoption. Lisa's reply was, "If the Lord wants me to adopt a baby he will send one to my house!" *The tongue has the power of life* (Prov. 18:21).

Within a few months a young lady brought her infant son, Noah, to the Artis' home, looking for a family to adopt him. A mutual friend had told the natural mother about the Artis' desires to have babies. The adoption process was quick and uncomplicated. Lisa and her husband were satisfied with the wonderful little boy God had given them but Lisa's gratification was temporary. She never failed to be grateful for her son, but she wanted, and had asked for a little girl, whom she would name Grace Alice. When Noah was almost three years old, Lisa began to experience the deep emotional longings again. Her arms would actually ache to hold her little girl. Shortly after Noah turned three years old, a very dear friend of Lisa's, who knew how Lisa longed for a little girl, notified her that a little girl would soon be available for adoption. Lisa's friend was in contact with the physician who expected to deliver a little girl within the week. The private adoption originally planned, had fallen through the cracks at the last minute. The natural mother did not want to go through an agency. Within a week Lisa and her husband picked up their baby daughter from the hospital. Lisa said she noticed that the longing had left. Her desire for children had reached a state of completion. For the first time in many years the emptiness that had almost become a part of her life was gone. She had reached fulfillment for her desire to have babies. The longing did not end until her desire was filled to completion. She was happy and grateful for her son, and she remains pleased with Noah and grateful to God for him, but she longed for a boy and a girl. When she got her girl, she no longer longed for babies!

When fulfillment comes you will know it. You may still long for many things but longings are specific. It is hard to know what it will take to bring a specific longing to completion when *you have no idea what you want.* It is possible, but not probable, that you might stumble upon the thing that will bring a specific longing to an end. It is not wise to drift in and out of relationships hoping that one of these days you will luck upon the right one that will fulfill your needs. One relationship may not be capable of fulfilling all of a person's needs. There may be a specific need to fellowship with family members, another need to communicate with social friends, and of course the desire to fellowship with a partner for life. Are you willing to take such chances with your emotions, intellectual abilities and other valuable assets? Until you are sure what is needed to fill the empty spaces within, you should wait. Use the time wisely and spend some time looking inside of yourself. Perhaps you are not so sure of what it would take to fulfill your desires because you are not really sure who you are. Many of the things you may be seeking from others may only be found within yourself.

If you are among the masses who are wondering, "What is there to know?" The answer is simple, there is everything to know. Do you know the origin of your character? Do you know that just as there are reasonable, healthy relationships there are also unreasonable, unhealthy relationships? Before making a commitment to someone to perform any specific task and become bound to someone emotionally and intellectually, take a little time to know what makes them form certain unfounded impressions. Learn when the first relationship begins for everyone and the affects first relationships can have on all future relationships. A brief visit to the basement where the foundations of life are laid could answer some unasked questions for you. Pause just long enough to get to know why you may be influenced by things and people that you do not wish to be identified with. This may enable you to better understand yourself as well as other people and some of the things that influences total behavioral patterns.

Chapter Three
IN THE BASEMENT

Filled with the newness of life was the beginning of my fate
I thought I heard a voice whispering, "Dear child, be still and
wait.
Life's many transitions will not take very long.
So stay down in the basement of life until you learn how to be
strong.

"Hello, world," think many newborn infants as they
breathe in their first breath of air in the new outside world. As
soon as their eyes are opened, they are met with many, many
new and different transitions all at once. They are surrounded
by unfamiliar voices, touched by unfamiliar hands, and for a
brief moment they probably seem lost in their new, vast
surroundings. They do the only thing they know how to do at
that moment. They curl their little bodies up into a semi-circle
and cry. They are probably longing to return to their former
place of comfort and familiarity. The swift transitions that the
whispering voice told them about did not take long. Suddenly
a familiar voice is heard! While they try to get a grip on life
and find the familiar voice, they are touched by familiar hands
that caress them as they count fingers and toes. Then they are
held close to their mother's warm body and they hear a
familiar heartbeat. They know that touch and the beat of that

heart because they were one with the body of their mother for as long as they can remember. When they feel a soft warm nipple nestle against their lips and they begin to suck in warm, satisfying liquid that fills their stomach, all their immediate needs are met. They feel safe and comfortable and develop a sacred feeling akin to worship and adoration for a person who made them feel safe and comfortable. Life in the outside world of almost every infant begins with love. This is where the very first relationship of life begins. Life will be filled with transition after transition after the initial outburst of emotions within the inner chambers of human life. Some of the changes will seem swift and others will evolve slowly. However, no one will be exempt from the alterations, variations and adjustments that comes with growth and development. Everything that the infant hears, sees, feels and experiences will become a part of his/her character. Children come into the world with all the equipment they need to build good character or develop poor traits. They are totally dependent on someone else to fulfill all of their needs and supply them with enough information to become independent in the future. Their first relationship is like a springboard for all future relationships. The basement of life, their beginning, is like a workshop. As they grow and develop from one phase to another, someone has to take them to the basement and prepare them, step-by-step, to meet the challenges, and teach them to share in the joys of life. They do not yet know how to behave appropriately. Learning how to interact with others and to grow up in the right direction is done in the basement of life

The basement of life is the workshop where modifications, alterations, adjustments and conversions takes place. Children must be ready to meet some of the simple challenges that they will be confronted with in the material world before they are sent up from the basement. When children are sent to the first floor unprepared, they are exposed to many different types of spirits that are just waiting for an opportunity to influence their minds. At first the hearts of children seem pure and innocent. They are trusting, loving and accepting of those with whom they come in contact on a regular basis. Usually, their souls have not experienced misery so they only know happiness and satisfaction. Their spirits are unaltered. In the unaltered state the spirit can easily be influenced and led astray, or it can be influenced to receive good, just, and right impressions. The mind is like an almost empty computer disc or an almost dry sponge. It has room for an entire life story to be written and can absorb everything to which it is exposed.

In the very beginning of life children begin to learn the principles that will affect what they perceive as right and wrong behavior. This is the perfect time for parents to begin to teach them to form good habits. They already have the inclination to form worldly habits. Their natural spirit is in tune with the attractions in the material world or that realm of sin controlled by Satan. Perhaps some of you may have noticed that children are more prone to learn things associated with the material world than they are to learn things that are beneficial to their development. The blueprints that will govern many of their impressions and perceptions will be handed down to them by their parents or caretakers. Children share something in common with all living things. They must be trained in the way they should grow. They will always grow and develop in accordance with their training. Lack of training or inappropriate training can and does have disastrous affects. Children will grow and develop. How they grow and develop will depend upon the work that is done in the basement of their lives. Children are like clay in many ways, like plants and other living things in other ways. They are in a position to be molded into any type of vessels. However, if they are permitted to use their own free choice, lack of wisdom and knowledge will cause them to become useless vessels. They have one or two ways to be molded. *Like clay in the hands of the potter, so are you in my hands* declares the Lord (Jer. 18:5). God can direct parents to shape children into vessels that seem best to Him. Parents who fail to participate in the molding of their children are also responsible for the marred vessel their children may become.

People who work with plants know that plants are at risk of being choked out by weeds and eaten up by insects unless they are given proper care. After the weeds have been pulled out and the plants have been treated with pesticides, some plants still want to choose their own directions in which to grow. Often a trellis or a stake has to be placed in the ground to support and to guide plants in the direction they should grow. It is no different with children. They are vulnerable and unprotected from the things within their environment. If they are left to go their own way, children will be like weeds that grow wild without any definite direction. Without adequate wisdom, knowledge and understanding, the adversary will gobble them up and lead them down paths of destruction. We see evidence of this in the newspapers and hear it on the six o'clock news daily. Young children are torturing, maiming and even murdering their peers over foolishness. Young minds that are not fed healthy, wholesome food at home will eat from anyone's table. Whatever they digest will be evident in the way they behave. A trellis or stake must be placed in the soil in which they are growing so that their young minds can grow in the desired direction. In Proverbs 22:6, King Solomon advised parents to, *train up a child in the way he should go and when he is old he will not depart from it.* Parents should consider it a blessing to take children down to the workshop so that they can learn how to adapt to appropriate and acceptable behavioral traits. It is much easier to train than it is to re-train. Many people wonder, "what is the right way?" Some even say that there is no right way to train a child. I'm glad you brought up the subject. King Solomon had some wonderful advice that has been tried, tested and trusted for many centuries and found to be effective.

Well-behaved children did not come into the world with more wisdom, knowledge and understanding than children who are not well behaved. The difference is what is done in the basement when parents have the authority and the control. *Folly is bound up in the heart of a child, but the rod of discipline will drive it out*(Prov. 22:15). The rod of discipline does not necessarily mean that physical punishment is needed to drive the foolish ideas and actions out of the hearts of all children. It simply means that all children are inquisitive and want to learn how things work in their environment. They do not know about consequences until they are taught. Discipline, or some corrective intervention will become necessary to teach them that every decision and action has a consequence consistent with behavior or decisions. At some point in inquisitive childrens' lives, when they are exposed to the influences of the adversary, they will be tempted to do something foolish that could be very dangerous to their well-being. Children learn how to manipulate adults, and assert themselves very, very early in life. Discipline will change the direction that they want to grow in. It is their nature and a part of their *job* as children to be foolish. It is a parent's responsibility to attempt to direct them away from foolishness. Discipline is one way of preventing some of them from following paths of destruction in the future. Discipline also imparts wisdom and promotes healthy and happy family relationships when it is rooted in love. Parents who love their children and are concerned with how they develop and behave do not balk at disciplinary practices. *He who spares the rod [or corrective practices] hates his son, but he who loves him is careful to discipline him* (Prov. 13:24). Every parent probably wants his/her children to be respected and respectable, liked and well-liked, but just wanting it to be so is not enough to make a difference. Once parents realize that there are forces of evil in the material world that will devour anyone who is unprotected, they might be motivated to take training, correcting and other disciplinary practices seriously. Children must be taught self-control so that they can avoid some of the pit falls of life. *Be self-controlled and alert. Your enemy the devil prowls around like a roaring lion looking for someone to devour* (I Pet. 5:8). Undisciplined children are easy prey. This is a very true statement that was proven by an experience that a colleague and I shared.

I worked very closely with George. He and his wife September had two wonderful sons for whom they had high hopes. September was acquainted with God and His powers. George had some reservations. One day George, who was always very upbeat, seemed very troubled about his oldest son

Seth's behavior. When I asked George about his troubled expression he said that Seth, who was about fifteen, had begun to defy every principle that he and September had ever reinforced in his life. He was beginning to stay out late at night and becoming involved in all kinds of bad behavior. Nothing George or September said or did made any difference. September and George were oblivious to the power and influences of the devil in their son's life. Seth had become involved with some gang members unknowingly and he had begun to adhere to their standards and follow the principles that they were guided by, which were different from the rules that governed good conduct. Seth had begun to listen to strange music and isolate himself from the family. He became belligerent and irritable. The onset, of Seth's new-found traits, was sudden.

George knew that I prayed daily, with two prayer partners, on an early morning prayer line. At his request, I contacted my prayer partners and we began to intercede for Seth according to Luke 10:19, *I have given you authority to trample on snakes and scorpions and to overcome the power of the enemy; nothing will harm you.* We knew that the scorpions and snakes were representatives of evil spirits in the material world. The enemy represents Satan himself who is always on the prowl. September was inspired to take Seth out of the enemy's territory and isolate him from the spirits that influenced his behavior. Although Seth was in the process of becoming a young man at a very rapid pace, September and George realized that they still had the authority and the responsibility to take him to the workshop in the basement and make some critical adjustments. It took some very serious and extremely hard disciplinary measures to prevent Seth from continuing to follow the path of destruction that he was traveling down at the time.

When George and September embraced the Spirit of God and permitted themselves to be directed by His inspirations, they were able to alter the course of Seth's development. They later learned that the path of destruction that Seth was traveling down was about to lead him into something that would have, negatively, altered his life forever. Seth's peers were incarcerated shortly after George and September removed him from the environment, where danger existed. George and September were glad that they followed the advice of King Solomon, *Discipline your son, for in that is hope; do not be a willing party to his death* (Prov. 19:18). Swift intervention and strict discipline enabled Seth to develop into a wonderful young man. He has thanked his parents many times for their wisdom and guidance.

Children who are disciplined bring peace to a parent's heart and delight to their souls. After months of anger and childish foolishness, Seth became a delight to his parents. Training children has to be among the priorities in life. There are many people who are more concerned about the training their pets receive than they are about their children's training. People become excited about their pets and become involved in disciplining them. Many dogs are sent to obedience school as soon as they are purchased so that a professional trainer can teach them how to behave in an acceptable manner. The trainer sets firm boundaries for all the animal in training. Each time the animal goes outside of the pre-determined limitations, it is met with disciplinary action to correct its behavior. When the animal responds in the desired manner, he is rewarded with a morsel of food, a pat on the head and word of encouragement. This process is repeated over and over and over until the animal learns how to behave according to a set of pre-determined rules. How much more important and intelligent are the children? This is the way to train children to behave according to accepted standards of good conduct. It is a long and tedious process but the rewards will be worth the effort. The number of emotionally wounded, undisciplined and unprincipled children who do not know how to solve simple and complex problems will be decreased. There will be fewer concerns about the relationships children and adults establish. Once children are trained properly, parents can feel more comfortable about how they will respond to the influences in the material world. Once children learn how to behave appropriately, they may stray away from their teachings on occasion. But as they grow older, they will probably explore many, many possibilities and suffer the consequences of them all. However, it is comforting to know that when they have the desire to do the right thing they will return to the training of their youth. They will at least know the right way to behave.

There are people who seem to love their children too much to discipline them. They do not want to hurt them or cause the children to think harshly of them. *He who spares the rod hates his son, but he who loves him is careful to discipline him* (Prov. 13:24). Proper discipline is rooted in love. It is love that enables parents to make right and just decisions regarding the type of discipline that will be effective for the children.

True love prevents a parent from punishing a child for purposes not related to discipline and training. Discipline promotes happy family relationships. Once children learn how to respond to order, principles and rules in the home among those whom they love, they know how to develop *relating skills* that will affect their lives for years to come. Good, healthy, relationships along with nurturing, training and discipline, build character, instill moral integrity and prepares children for other relationships that they will begin to encounter very early in life. That is probably one reason God permitted parents and children to spend quality time in the basement of life together while the child is soft enough to mold, resilient enough to alter and innocent enough to trust.

Frustrated, emotionally wounded adults, who do not know how to behave according to the accepted standards of right and wrong, are usually products of undisciplined, undernourished child-parent relationships. Children need and want boundaries set for them and rules to regulate their behavior. They want to behave in an acceptable manner, and most of all they want to please their parents. When boundaries are defined and acceptable behavioral practices are reinforced on a consistent basis, children feel secure and loved. They crave attention and will stop at nothing to get it. They learn to assert themselves by attempting to exceed the limitations of the boundaries set for them. If they are permitted to do so continuously, they grow up believing that they can be assertive enough in other relationships to exceed other boundaries without consequences. It is never too early to begin to train children in the right way. Missed opportunities can never be regained.

Most parents who experienced physical, emotional or social pain and embarrassment as children usually inflict the same pain and embarrassment on their own children. It is usually not because they do not remember their unhealthy experiences or they want to punish their children unduly, but because they do not know any other way to perform. Their parents' behavior was probably retained within their memory as right behavior. When children learn that their parents' behavior was harmful, some of them do not have the courage to admit that they were emotionally, physically, or socially wounded by their parents. They will try to rationalize their parents' behavior or deny that such incidents ever occurred. However, until they acknowledge their pain and its cause, they cannot begin to deal with it. Computers and the human mind have many similarities. They both retain information that is made available to them. Only the data that was put into the mind or the computer can be brought up on the "screen." If the mind encounters situations that it needs to respond to, it responds to the impressions and experiences associated with that situation. Personal impressions have nothing to do with reason or right behavior. People respond to impressions in accordance with their own personal knowledge and experiences, right or wrong. What children perceive as right does not change unless changes are made in the data that they have stored in their minds. People respond to what they feel and believe. Wounded emotions are unhealthy so they motivate people to respond in an unhealthy manner. People can only respond to things in the manner that is familiar to them. The way people respond, or the impressions they have, usually have nothing to do with intellect or educational background. I knew a very intelligent woman who seemed to have her life all together but some of the decisions that she made seemed different and unusual to me. Her story is a good example of a person responding to her impression of right and wrong in accordance with her upbringing and not according to her educational background and capacity to receive, retain and process information.

Julia was very attractive, well educated and working in a high-profile position as an administrative assistant for a major oil company. She was a divorced mother of two children, Jan who was a freshman in college and Jon who was about to enter high school. She had sole custody of her children. She and her children's father had a wonderful relationship and they shared the responsibility of the children with no major problems. Julia met a man, Steve, and decided to marry him and move across country with him. She informed her ex-husband that he would have to take Jon to live with him. Jon was very angry and frustrated. He told Julia that he needed her in his life on a consistent basis. Jan was also upset because she had enrolled in a college near her hometown to be near her mother. Neither child had ever been separated from Julia for any length of time. Julia had decided that it was time for her to live her own life. She had no problem leaving her children behind. Years went by and Julia's children formed relationships of their own; however, they both felt somewhat detached from their significant others. Jan was married with two children. She would occasionally go out with her friends and stay away for days before returning home. Jon got married but did not feel attached to his wife and child. The relationship ended in divorce before he celebrated his first anniversary. Years went by before Julia got up enough courage and had enough faith in God to come to terms with her role in her children's impressions of healthy relationships.

When Julia was very young her own mother, Angie, just got up and left her and her younger brother with their father. Years went by before she saw her mother again. She did not develop a good parent-child relationship with her mother until her mother was quite old.

During one of her heart-to heart talks with her mother she asked the question that had plagued her for years,"why did you leave us?" Her mother told her she did not know any better at that time. Julia's grandmother had left Angle when she was very young to work as a live-in housekeeper. The cycle of abandonment had repeated itself through three generations. The information retained within the minds of Angie, Julia, Jan and Jon concerning abandonment came up on the "screen of their minds" as right and appropriate behavior. Julia said she always felt like something was missing in her life. It was probably that"mother-wit," that no one but a mother or mother figure can give. It is an innate form of intelligence that comes from experiencing a healthy relationship with one's mother or mother figure. Julia said she only found the courage to face her mother in love after she formed a personal relationship with God. Once she felt good enough about herself to come out of denial and face reality, she could confront her own mother in love. She did not feel peaceful and secure enough to begin the healing process until she forgave her mother. Once Julia came to terms with her own behavior she was able to seek forgiveness from her children.

The parent-child relationship is established long before children learn about God. Parents are like gods to their children until they learn to worship God or some other gods.

The parent-child relationship began long before children learned about God or any other gods, Some children never lose their attitude of worship towards their parents. It is difficult for them (at any age) to believe that their parents were wrong, mistaken or dishonest. Sometimes when children learn that their parents are less than perfect they become suspicious of everyone they meet. When the relationship between parents and their children is threatened other people may suffer that are not a part of that relationship. The time parents' spend with their children in the basement is short lived. It would be wise for parents to take full advantage of that time.

Many relationships suffer when the true, tried and tested standards that worked previously, seem to be in a constant state of adjustment. Agencies seem to adjust pre-determined standards to suit the needs of a society without values or control. Some of the adjustments that had an adverse affect on the way people behave include, taking prayer out of schools and forbidding parents to control the way they disciplined their children. When prayer went out of the schools, in came guns and all manner of evil behavior. When governmental agencies decided to give children the authority to intervene in their parents' disciplinary actions, the authority was taken away from parents. This compromise has created a huge problem in the way some parents relate to their children and the way children relate to parents. Responsibility without authority defeats the purpose of discipline. Children use the adjustments to strip their parents of authority and control by threatening to report their parents' activities to the agencies that control the laws of the land. Enough good, respectable parents have been arrested and spent much time, energy and esources trying to prove they had the right to discipline an unruly child to send a message that children are in control. It is unreasonable for anyone to believe that a child who does not know how to behave responsibly or make logical decisions based on reality and fact can decide when discipline is unwarranted. To some children, any form of discipline is too harsh. *Whoever loves discipline loves knowledge, but he who hates correction is stupid* (Prov 12:1). The deeds of an undisciplined child will show up in his behavior at some point and time in his/her life.

Some people are still in bondage to some of the decisions that were made for them before they were held accountable. When people are in a position to make their own decisions, they do not have to allow former decisions to affect their lives and the way they relate to themselves and others. Feelings of inadequacy and other negative feelings are responsible for strongholds in many peoples' lives. Personal feelings about what others will think cause many people to conceal things that they had no control over.

The first relationship people enter into will leave lasting impressions on the minds of many people. Children who were nurtured in wholesome, healthy environments often believe that everyone else came from similar family backgrounds. Adults rarely get an opportunity to know what was done in the basement of the lives of the people they meet as adults. The emotional health of everyone is affected by the nurturing they received in the basement of life. The emotional health of people is also affected by the lack of nurturing received in the basement of life. Relationships are affected by the emotional health of the people who enter into them. All one can do is spend enough time observing the character of those with whom they plan to enter into relationships.

Chapter Four

IS THERE A PROBLEM HERE?

*If within your heart, pain and darkness is all that you can see
and your soul seems bound in chains and your spirit is not
free.*
*Your silence may give consent, but not to the fullness of love
and divine power to bring peace from the Holy One above.*

There are people who are functioning in numerous types
of relationships who are not capable of sharing their interests,
purposes and activities with them. They may go through the
motions of sharing in some of the activities of others, but
because they are "married" to emotional pain they *cannot*
actually form ties that bind them to other people. Emotionally
painful people *want* to share in the joys and sorrows of their
mates, friends and associates, but their "containers" for
sharing are already filled to capacity with their own pain and
concerns. They may verbally express love, commitment,
respect, and other qualities that make-up healthy, sound
relationships; however, within their hearts, souls, and spirits
their pain is their constant companion. It always takes priority
over anyone or anything else. Emotionally painful people have
profound needs for relief on a continuous basis. Their entire
hearts, souls, spirits, and minds are pre-occupied with seeking

relief. Most of the time, their impressions of their needs become so profound that they are driven to behave in extremely inappropriate ways to obtain relief. Their impressions are disconnected from their level of intelligence, educational background, social status, or professional performance. A classic example of a well-educated, intelligent, professional person's inappropriate behavior [seemingly without restraints] has been played out on the big screen of life before the entire world. The highest political officer in this nation has brought shame and embarrassment to his family and put his future and this nation in jeopardy for a few moments of pleasure. He probably believed that he deserved whatever temporary relief he sought. Our president is certainly not uneducated, unintelligent, unsociable, or incapable of performing his duties. Obviously, his impression of his need for satisfaction took priority over everything else in his life probably because of inner pain. He is not alone in responding to his perceived needs inappropriately.

Many, many good, fun-loving, well-educated, professional people suffer from damaged or wounded emotions. Others who witness the effects that inappropriate behavior have on people, rarely know or even think about the causes of their pain. The effects of peoples' emotional pain are present in every walk of life. These effects harm many well-adjusted, emotionally healthy, unsuspecting people continuously. Perhaps if one knew a little about the characteristic traits of emotionally wounded people he/she may choose to make different decisions about establishing new, close, personal relationships.

Pain, frustrations, fears and secrets hidden in the darkest corners of a person's mind are all excess baggage that they carry around from one relationship to another. People can become servants to some of their hidden emotions. Once they become servants, they are not emotionally free to form healthy relationships with anyone else. They are controlled by their pain. Most of them really want to be free from the invisible chains that bind them to their emotional wounds. But they are not sure what to do, where to begin, how to be set free or what awaits them on the other side. The pain that most emotionally wounded people experience is a major part of their make-up. Many, many adults are still being held captive to emotional wounds that occurred in the early stages of their childhood. Some of the issues that continue to cause them emotional distress were not their fault. As children, it was hard for them to separate themselves from the problems that surrounded them. This is especially true if physical and emotional pain, anxiety, humiliation and fear were the outcome. If the wounds were inflicted by parents, close family members or others whom children loved and trusted, the children usually believed that they were at fault and not the person who actually inflicted the pain. Ultimately they do not like themselves very much in the beginning. They think "something must be wrong with me."

Most children hate to be edifferent or excluded from the activities and interests of their peers. If they are abused, neglected, or ignored they view themselves as less worthy than others. They believe their abusers' behavior will ultimately set them apart from their peers. Emotionally wounded children learn very early in life to change reality by replacing the unacceptable things in their lives with wishful thinking as a means of self-protection. Sometimes reality is just too painful for them to cope with. They learn to imitate the lifestyles of others whom they perceive as perfect. They verbally, and sometimes mentally, create a type of family life that makes them seem important. Whenever they talk about the people who caused their pain, they speak about profound affection and attention showered upon them by those persons. They always know about life on the edge of reality because they go home to their real lives where unpleasant or painful experiences occur. They get a temporary reprieve when they enter into a state of denial. For many adults, the temporary relief becomes an almost permanent delay. Denial, deception and erroneous self-identification become a way of life that continue throughout adulthood. The longer one denies reality, the harder it becomes to face facts about reality and one's lack of healthy emotional development. After long periods of time, anger and resentment become a springboard for many of the things the person does in life to bring pleasure, or validate his/her worth. This is how they cope with the things that they have survived. Most adults continue to be too afraid to admit to their parents or trusted abusers at any age that they are suffering ill effects from their wounds or up-bringing.

Most people seem to be more protective of negligent, indifferent and abusive parents than are people who were raised in wholesome, healthy environments. Emotionally wounded children try harder to get their parents' love and attention. Emotionally healthy children usually do not have to put forth much effort to get their parents' attention and love. People who never received love and acceptance from their parents look to others for appreciation, merit or self-worth.

All unhealthy emotional responses are not caused by abuse or neglect. There are many other issues that cause people emotional distress that affects how people relate to others.

Sometimes the issues that provoked emotional pain in some people may seem minor to others who are not suffering from the impact of those same consequences. However, to the person suffering ill-effects, the issues were major at the time they occurred. To children, anything that isolated them from their peers was painful. All emotional wounds were not inflicted by parents or family members or even close associates. Many children were wounded by their peers. Some adults still suffer emotionally from being overweight as children or from wearing glasses, dressing differently, following different religious practices, or low family status. There are numerous things that caused children to be labeled as "different" by their peers that humiliated them and created an environment for low self-esteem. Some adults never rose above the taunts and teasing experiences. They carried their pain into their close adult relationships. Many of those childhood experiences still affect some adults' abilities to establish and maintain close relationships based on reality and total commitment. They always think others will think less of them if they knew their secrets. Many people who are in pain attempt to compensate by acts of deception. They need inner assurance that they have some value.

Numerous people are driven to excel professionally to prove to themselves and others that they are worthy of recognition and acceptance. There is probably no limit to the number of people functioning in high-profile positions of authority who are suffering from the effects of old emotional wounds. They are driven by their longings and cravings to meet some of their many unmet needs. However, needs and longings are specific. Some of their longings and cravings continue to go unmet as they climb higher and higher up the ladder of success because they cannot always identify what they really need. They may experience moments of temporary gratification through transient relationships but they are not free to form ties that will bind them to anyone. Emotionally wounded people always need to feel included and have their egos stroked. Because hurting people are different, they choose different methods of boosting their egos and feeling included. Some seek acceptance from other needy people who are like them in many ways. They share sad stories about how the world has mistreated them, but rarely identify the real problems. They seem to feed off each other's pain. Hurting people are looking for some means of escape or relief. They are always in motion. They are either running from pain or running towards a sense of pleasure or fulfillment.

People experience pain in varying degrees. They seek pleasure and relief according to who they are and what is available to them. Some people become work-aholics and attempt to drown their problems in their work. Others may use alcohol or drugs to numb the pain. Some people choose to join gangs with others who "understand and sympathize" with them. They associate with other people who create mayhem in an effort to prove to society that they are worthy of "respect" and recognition. They do not seem to fear death. It is usually life that most gang members seem to fear. They fear the pain and anxiety that they wake up to and go to sleep to on a day-to-day basis. Most of them do not know love because they have never experienced love and acceptance. They respond to hate and evil dealings because that is what they know. Within the heart, soul, and spirit of every hurting individual there will probably be many similarities to others who have been hurt, no matter what their financial or social status may be. Pain has no respect for personal status. Some wounds may be deeper or more recent than others but they all cause pain in the innermost chambers of a person's being. No one can see or touch this pain with the natural eye, or hand but the hurting people know that it is there. The effects are displayed in the drastic changes within our society.

The emotional wounds of hurting people have the potential to affect almost anyone who is emotionally healthy. Emotionally healthy and unhealthy people cross paths on a regular basis. They are both looking for someone to share portions of their lives with. Both may wear Brooks Brothers' suits or St. John Knits or they may shop in the same bargain basement together. They may be on the same social calendars, or attend the same worship services. They work side-by-side in every profession. Emotionally healthy and unhealthy people associate with each other in every walk of life. There is no way that anyone can look at a person and know that he/she is in emotional pain. Most emotionally wounded people are masters of deception so it may seem almost impossible to differentiate them from anyone else. However, a practical understanding of some of the subtle, but recognizable traits that are characteristic of emotionally wounded people may lend some valuable insights to emotionally healthy people.

People who are dealing with painful issues within the inner chambers of their minds cannot get past their pain. The need or fulfillment of some of the basics things that most people take for granted, such as acceptance, value, and nurturing, seem to eat away at hurting people from the inside out. These needs do not go away if they are not met. People who have never experienced love are not familiar enough with love to recognize it when it is offered to them. Hurting people are so accustomed to protecting their feelings from further harm that they become self-absorbed. They give very little of themselves to others and permit very few of other peoples' interests to enter into their lives. They think that their needs are more important than the needs of anyone else. While they may excel professionally, their personal lives and immediate family lives may suffer. Anything that forces attention away from them and towards something or someone else will not hold their interest very long. Most of the things that they think are significant are things that enhance their own importance, power or reputation. They want to think that they are important and they want everyone else around them to think that they are important. Their outward regard for themselves is usually selfish and unwholesome but inwardly their feelings may actually include inadequacy and self-loathing.

Outward appearance plays a pivotal role in the lives of hurting people because they are superficial and believe that others pay particular attention to their mode of dress and mannerism. They are often misled by their own illusions of themselves. They are like "Charlie Tuna" in an old commercial for Sun-Kist Tuna, who declared that (because he thought he looked good), "Star-Kist is going to call me." However, Star-Kist assured the audience that they wanted tuna that tasted good. They were not concerned with the way the fish looked. In the minds of emotional hurting people, they have not only denied their most painful realities, like "Charlie Tuna" they go a step further and replace them with more pleasant incidents. Some people actually begin to believe their own erroneous versions of what actually occurred to harm them emotionally. In reality they *wanted* things to be different. By shuffling their memories of what actually occurred to them, many people have mistaken concepts of things that caused them pain. All mistaken concepts do not necessarily cause emotional harm but they can prevent people from facing realities and getting on with their lives. People are prone to remember things the way they wanted them to be, especially if some of the things they experienced were unpleasant or just unsatisfactory.

All selfish people are not emotionally wounded, but most emotionally wounded people are selfish. Many people who have unresolved conflicts and other issues that prevent them from bonding with others and getting on with their lives are suffering from their own false beliefs and impressions as was the case with a young lady I knew who shared her experience with me,

March grew up in the same household as her sister April. They were guided by the same principles and disciplined for similar acts of disobedience. March and April's parents were poor in material possessions and poorly educated. They never learned good management skills. Maybe they could have managed their finances better, but they just did not know how. They loved their children and provided them with the necessities of life, and on occasion, they gave them some of the things they wanted. April never felt unloved or unaccepted by her parents. As soon as March began to see how people who had more expendable cash flows lived, she decided that she wanted to live that way. In her heart she began to resent her parents' lack of finances and education. They just did not measure up to her friends' parents. March began to associate with people she wanted to be like. April and March were very good friends and shared many of their dreams and secrets.

April did not notice March's growing resentment of their financial and social status, or lack of it until they were much older. April wanted her lifestyle to be different too. She began to baby sit and iron for others to earn extra money to buy some of the things she wanted. March began to develop superior airs and create a lifestyle that did not exist. March seemed to resent her parents and misrepresent some of the things they did as well as some of the things they failed to do.

On several occasions, when March and April were talking about their childhood, March made comments about things that happened when they were children that just never really happened. March was always either the center of attention or the injured party, whichever role she decided was more to her liking at the time. Being poor was an issue that March never got past. Often she claimed that they were hungry but April always remembered having plain, filling food but nothing fancy, unless it was a holiday or something very special going on. When she tried to correct March there was a clashing of the minds. April remembered being poor but she also remembered being happy most of the time. She remembered lots of laughing and kidding around in their household. She also remembered March being head strong and stubborn. March's impression of herself as a child was that she was passive and quiet.

March began to deny herself many of the pleasures of life at a time when she could have afforded many of the things she dreamed about. She feared being poor. She saved her money and skimped on clothes, food and other things that she once coveted. However, she always splurged when she was with her friends and acquaintances who had professional presence. Her friends and acquaintances were under the impression that she was a person of means, which in reality she was. However, she cheated herself out of many things that she really, really wanted because she did not think she could afford them and maintain her "nest egg" that she was forever building up. April had far fewer resources than March, but she enjoyed life to the fullest on a day-by-day basis. March seemed bitter about her impressions and her own illusions of her life. Somehow, March's family never quite lived up to her ideals of what they should or could have done. She was never confident that her parents did their best with what they had. She always compared them to the parents of her friends. They never measured up. All of her disappointments and failures in her life were blamed on her parents. March never faced reality. In her mind she was right and all other views were wrong. She continues to deal with some issues that were real, but perhaps magnified a bit, as well as issues that she created in her own mind. These issues have kept March emotionally bound.

It does not matter how the issues came into existence, if they cause problems within the heart, soul, and spirit of a person, they must be dealt with in the same way one deals with emotional wounds.

The underlying causes of the pain and issues that keep people in bondage will also prevent them from bonding with anyone else in any type of relationship. Their issues are packed up and taken from one relationship to another until the person decides that he/she is ready to face reality and be set free. Emotionally hurting people are needy and are fervently seeking gratification, temporary relief and enough of a reprieve to get them through another day. Sometimes they become overburdened by their pain and take their frustrations out on the person with whom they feel safe. Many emotionally hurting people suddenly give vent to their emotions by doing or saying something bizarre. Once the explosion is over, the need for ventilation is appeased for the moment. Usually, if the person that they used as a sounding board brings up their behavior again, the wounded person is likely to deny that the explosion ever occurred. Emotionally wounded people are neither mean nor unintelligent. They go out of their way to do things for others when they can take credit for their actions or receive some adulation. Most of the things that they do involves themselves first. Everyone and everything else is secondary. They are conceited and forever seeking praise and recognition to cover up their true feelings. Outwardly they have a selfish regard for their personal advantages and interests. They have no qualms about telling others, "I *need* you to do this for *me* now!" Some of them are so full of that person they seem to be that there is no room inside for anyone else. They believe they deserve the best that life has to offer at anyone's expense.

Society dictates that internal pain is associated with one's mental state of mind. It leads people to believe that emotional wounds tend to make a person mentally unbalanced. This could not be further from the truth. Society's attitude regarding emotional pain is one of the major reason so many people suffer in silence and *inner darkness is all that they can see.* People readily accept physical pain and embrace the injured parties. Emotional pain may be more unbearable and easier to treat than some physical "dis-eases." Both types of pain disrupt the ease necessary for peace, harmony and joy in the lives of those who are suffering. When people are in physical pain, others expect them to c ry out for someone to lend their assistance in relieving the pain. An analgesic usually brings temporary relief but does nothing to help the underlying cause. Once relief is achieved, a person's attitude, disposition and overall personality may change until the affects of the analgesic wear off. People do not function very well when they are in any kind of pain. People with emotional pain are condemned to suffer in silence. They put forth every effort to conceal the pain from anyone who would judge them by the standards society has set. However, the pain is usually in control of the person, depending on its severity. Emotionally wounded people must cry out but they cry out in different ways. Some cry out by behaving inappropriately in the dark places of life. Seemingly insatiable sexual appetites or excessive use of alcohol are more acceptable by today's society than the causes and effects of emotional pain. Hurting people want something that will shut out the inner world of pain in which they live. Many of the things that hurting people indulge in are done in excess because they do not have the control as they would like for people to think they have. They are looking for relief from their pain just as emotionally healthy people seek relief from physical pain. They just choose different types of "analgesics" to get immediate relief. Once they get the relief they are seeking, they can function until the affects wear off.

It is important for emotionally healthy people to be aware of who is crossing their pathways constantly looking for gratification through relationships. People who are looking for some ties that can bind them to someone else in a relationship should know that emotionally wounded people are slaves, prisoners, and servants to their pain. Until they are set free they cannot form ties that bind them to anyone. It is not as simple as "just wanting to change." This is not something that other people can "fix" by loving people in pain enough or accepting them as they are. Freedom and change are not impossible, but only the person who is bound can make that decision to change, based on his/her genuine desire and commitment to go through a long healing process. The wounded person has to make the decision to come out of denial and face reality. He or she must be ready to take his/her own personal self-discovery journey. All an emotionally healthy person can do is make a commitment to be a partner or support person who will help the wounded person through the process. Now anyone can make a decision to establish a relationship with someone who is self-centered, self-deceived, and therefore, deceiving of others. Once the decision is made, it may not be feasible to back out of the relationship. If the idea is to make things right for the wounded person it may be a downhill battle unless that person is ready to make some changes. The only decision an emotionally healthy person can make when he/she is committed, heart, soul and spirit to a relationship like that, is to learn how to maintain the relationship and maintain his/her own principles and moral integrity at the same time.

Dealing with one's own emotional pain is drastically different from trying to deal with someone else's inward pain. Helping someone through the healing process is no easy task. The support person must be committed to go through the entire process and provide a healthy example for the person who is suffering. It would help if the support person is a believer who can draw strength and patience from God. Emotional wounds must be healed before the hurting person can be emotionally whole, sound and healthy. The amount of time it takes to complete the process will depend upon the severity of the wound and the commitment of the hurting person and support person to stay the course. Emotional health comes when the pain has subsided.

Healing is a step-by-step process that begins with acknowledging that there is pain as well as the underlying cause of the initial wounds. Both the emotionally wounded person and the support person should understand that the healing process will probably be a long, painful experience, but a very necessary process if healing and freedom is to occur. The injured person must make a clean, clear affirmation of what he/she believes the origin of the pain is and confess the methods used to deal with the cause and effects of their wounds. Sometimes disclosing those things that have been hidden for a period of time is as painful as the actual incident. This is one of the most difficult steps in the process. Reliving such painful incidents may be too embarrassing for the person to disclose at one time. The support person should not be judgmental but respond with compassion if a response is necessary. In essence, the hurting person is exposing himself and his secrets to someone else. An emotionally wounded person cannot handle such a trying process alone. He/she needs an emotionally stable person to support him/her. It is impossible for one emotionally injured person to help another through the healing process. It is like the blind leading the blind. *If a blind man leads a blind man, both will fall into a pit* (Mat. 15:14). Confession is like a soothing balm that brings some relief but it only gets the healing process started. Both the support person and the wounded person should understand from the beginning, what the goal is. The goal should be restoration and freedom from bondage. Before restoration can take place, everything must be brought out of darkness and into the light. Partial truths only hinder the healing process. When people confess their faults one to another and pray for each other, healing can be made effective in a more powerful way according to James 5: 19&17.

Confession is stating exactly what happened, the conditions under which things happened, and how those things made the wounded person feel. The wounded person also states what he/she did as a result of the abuse, neglect, or whatever caused the problem. If deception, selfishness, hostility, anger, or hatred was the way a person dealt with the pain, that should be verbalized. Confession is not very pretty but, it can be cleansing, and it must be real.

Confession is followed by forgiveness. There are many ways to deal with forgiveness. One is, to have a face-to-face encounter with the perpetrator, if that is possible. Face-to-face encounters are not always probable. This method can be counter-productive. Forgiveness can also be done by writing down the complete confession and verbalizing it to someone and expressing a desire to forgive the perpetrator. The process of forgiveness involves renouncing anger, resentment, fear, anxiety, hostility and all the qualities that motivates a person to be selfish and driven to prove his/her self worth. Some people choose to write down all their painful memories and how they were inflicted. Once they honestly make their confession, they burn the paper. The ashes are used as a symbol of the dissolution of their pain. There is a divine method of receiving deliverance from emotional pain and forgiveness for the methods used to deal with the pain. *If we claim to be without sin, we deceive ourselves and the truth is not in us. If we confess our sins, He [God, through Jesus Christ] is faithful and just and will forgive us of our sins and purify us from all unrighteousness (Jn. 1:8-9).* Any negative thing a person does, think, or say about anyone interrupts that person's ability to communicate with God. The wounded person, seeking deliverance from God, must not deny that their immoral actions are sinful. He/she must also receive forgiveness before communication with God can be restored. Forgiveness is the key that unlocks the chains that bind people to their emotional pain. Emotionally wounded people who really, really want to be set free, *must* be real about going through the healing process. They must have a desire to be set free. Freedom only comes when the demons that hold people captive are gone out of their lives. The demons will put forth every effort to prevent, kill, steal, and destroy everything that can lead wounded people out of bondage. Jesus promises,*If you hold my teachings....then you will know the truth and the truth will set you free (Jn. 8:31-32).* The problem is, the adversary **does not want anyone to be set free.** As long as people remain in bondage they are just slaves, prisoners and servants to Satan and to their own emotions. Prisoners *cannot* set themselves free. Someone on the outside of their feelings and activities, with more authority than the adversary must become involved. Freedom from any type of bondage through forgiveness was very costly for God, who is the only One with more power than the adversary. The price for everyone's forgiveness was paid for through the agonizing death of Jesus, God's only Son, on Calvery's mountain! It was paid with His blood when He was pierced in the side on the cross! Jesus can give anyone the power to overcome the adversary, who controls the demons that keep you in bondage.

Jesus tells His disciples, *I have given you authority to overcome all the power of the enemy* (Lk. 10:19). No one knows humiliation like Jesus knew humiliation on His way to the cross. He forgave His perpetrators so that everyone else would be able to forgive their perpetrators. People must believe that they are capable of forgiving their perpetrator(s). Perhaps some hurting people may need more time, more power, or a conversion experience, before they are ready and capable of going through the healing process.

This is the deal. Forgiveness begins in the heart where the will to make decisions and meet, accept or reject God's word arises. Once the heart feels sorrow for the person that one wants to forgive, it makes the impression clear within that person's mind. The true feeling of sorrow precedes the act of forgiving. Hurting people may be thinking,"Why should I feel sorry for someone who caused me so many problems? They should be feeling sorry for me!" Well, there are several reasons to feel sorrow for them. They were probably doing what they knew to do. Perhaps they were slaves to emotional distress themselves. They may be in more pain than you are. However, this is not about them. It is about you and your freedom.

When people feel sorrow within their hearts, forgiveness is usually a response to that emotional feeling. Before verbally confessing, the mind must be conditioned to release the resentment, anger, frustration and any other negative feelings towards the person who is to be forgiven. Let it go! Letting go means taking the person(s) off the hook. Once the perpetrators have been taken off the hook, they can no longer be blamed for the hurting person's responses to past or present events. If

101

establish a relationship with his/her perpetrator, the relationship should be free from the negative feelings that held the wounded person captive. Amicable relationships between the abused and/or neglected and the abuser is not always possible and it is not necessary in order for healing to take place. Once a person has forgiven others they can ask for forgiveness for themselves. Jesus said He would *forgive us our debts as we have forgiven our debtors. If you forgive men when they sin against you, your heavenly Father will also forgive you. But if you do not forgive men their sins, your Father will not forgive your sins* (Mat. 6:12). Even after forgiveness of the perpetrator has taken place within the heart, freedom may be short lived unless the negative feelings are replaced with positive feelings. *When an evil spirit comes out of a man it goes through arid [barren, uninterested] places seeking rest and does not find it. Then it says,"I will return to the house I left." When it arrives, and finds the house unoccupied, swept clean and put in order. Then it goes and takes with it seven other spirits more wicked than itself and they go and live there. The final condition is worst than the first* (Mat. 12:44). The adversary wants you back as soon as you are set free. He will do anything to incarcerate you again. Forgetting may not come immediately, and for some it may never come at all. Whether a person can forget what happens or not, it would not be advantageous for the person to permit the painful memories to occupy his/her thought processes any more. When thoughts of the pain returns, the recovering person has choices. He/she can choose to use the new skills acquired while going through the healing process.

Total forgiveness, and the power to keep the body, mind, or house from being invaded by evil spirits, takes supernatural power. Whether an emotionally injured person seeks God or not, will depend upon their impression and real knowledge about Him. Remember, as an adult, most of the things that occur in life are the consequence of the decisions people made or failed to make. Embracing godly principles and beliefs involves decision making. With the power of God on a person's side the healing process can certainly be made easier to bear. Without Him it may be close to impossible to complete the process without going back into bondage again.

Even people who have established a relationship with God may become spiritually wounded and suffer spiritual pain. People have left the church and abandonded godly principles because of something someone said, did or failed to say or do. Some "believers" get angry with God and decide to turn their backs on Him! It does not matter what the cause of the spiritual injury is, that person has a need to be restored. God will not come after anyone. Remember, anyone can exercise his/her will to make a decision to follow God or abandon His ways and teachings at any time. It will be up to the person to choose, by his/her will, to return to the fold. Spiritually wounded people must go through the same healing process as emotionally wounded individuals. They have the advantage of One with supernatural power on their side, However, it is necessary for their support person to be a steadfast believer who knows how to pray and rightly divide the word of truth.

The support person for emotionally wounded people must be steadfast as well. He/she must be patient and wait for the wounded person to experience love, honesty, loyalty and acceptance. Once all the negative feelings have been released the person will need a safe, comforting, loving environment in which to recuperate. The process may seem long and tedious but the end results may be well worth the time and energy spent. Many things must occur before a person is whole, sound, healed and healthy. The signs of restoration include inward changes, feelings of value, and feelings of acceptance and love. The real attitude changes will comes after the inward changes take place. Some examples of the healed person's new attitude will include, feelings of inward pleasures in the simple things that life has to offer and the absence of hostility and indignation. The healed person will lose the attitude of self-centeredness and become concerned with the interests, activities and purposes of other people. That person will no longer have a need to prove anything to anyone and he/she will not be driven by demons or old destructive behaviors anymore.

Most people who have been set free from emotional wounds feel a need to help others who are in bondage. Once a person enjoys the benefits of freedom, he/she is not likely to go into bondage again. For the wounded person to remain free, the evil spirits must be overpowered by a being with more power than they possess. However, if a person is in the process of returning to old responses and behavioral traits he/she should repeat the healing process. The healing process can be repeated as often as the need arises.

It is important to know up front whether the person you endeavor to enter into a relationship with is emotionally healthy or emotionally wounded. Every partner, friend, or associate will not be capable of going through the healing process with anyone. Anyone who wishes to form ties that bind them to someone else should spend some time observing the characteristic traits with the person before making a commitment.

Chapter Five

TIES THAT BIND

Someone to call upon, anytime day or night
with news of some sorrow or a wonderful testimony in sight.
Someone with whom your sharing will never seem to end
is a treasured family member and a very close friend.

The thought of establishing a relationship with someone that you genuinely like, and who you believe likes you, is a pure joy and somewhat refreshing to almost anyone. Even preserving or sustaining relationships with special family members and long-time friends can be filled with excitement. In this twenty-first century world, relationships between family members and friends who are scattered all over the nation can be expensive and require real commitment. But the precious times shared between friends and family are more than worth the effort. True friends and loving family members are not separated within their hearts, souls, and spirits by time and distance. Even when the fellowship is not constant the relationship does not suffer.

Many relationships between family members, who are also friends, are very unique and special, especially among family members who are from the"old school." In yesteryears, family life and social life were intertwined where most families were

105

concerned. Family life usually meant that there was lways a constant support system in place. Everyone encouraged everyone else. They shared in each other's joys and sorrows and generally enjoyed each other's company. Families were much more than groups of people who shared similar genetic make-up and a common ancestry. They literally shared hopes, dreams, aspirations, disappointments, and every other aspect of their lives, with each other. Many of them may have had fewer resources than a great number of families have today so they had to share each other's space whether they wanted to or not. Sometimes the children shared beds with each other. Some of them looked forward to having someone to share their secrets with in the middle of the night or someone to confess their fears and anxieties to. Character building and a family's reputation was extremely important in yesteryears. Children's behavior reflected on the parent's training so children were trained by every adult they came in contact with. They learned love and respect from their elders as well as from their family members. Families were usually very protective of each other [especially the older members, who were protective of the younger ones]. There seemed to have been more two parent families than single-parent families in those days. Both parents were usually actively involved in the nurturing process. Families seemed much larger and dwelling places seemed much smaller. There were few things that separated families within the same household.

There was always work to do but there was also enough time do everything that needed to be done. Parents talked more with their children, their neighbors, friends and relatives one-on-one. Adults cooked and took food to anyone who was ill, and sometimes did chores while they were there. This was before the era of microwave ovens and many of the new inventions developed to make life easier and give families more time to spend with each other. Many times they took a child or two along to teach them how to visit the sick. It just seemed like days were longer and times were so much more enjoyable among families. Children were not rushed into growing up and making decisions for themselves before they were mature enough to make decisions based on knowledge and experience. When people were always in each other's faces, they learned to make the best of their situations and learned to love and even like each other. Sharing was a major part of the lessons that families taught by example. Mothers, fathers, older sisters and brothers were role models in those days. Families established good relationships among themselves that were often passed down from generation to generation. Some family members established close ties among themselves that made them friends. Some of those friendships were and remain almost sacred.

People establish relationships with social friends for many reasons but mostly for companionship. Occasionally the paths of people will cross who may seem to have a "magnetic self-likeness" that seem to draw them to each other. Within the inward chambers of the beings of these people they may feel like they must get to know each other better. That is often the beginning of a long relationship between social friends. When this occurs, and it may not occur often, getting to know each other proves to be almost fantastic. Their mental connection, interest, activities and purpose may be so similar that getting acquainted may seem like a self-discovery experience. Relationships between social friends are governed by the same standards by which almost all relationships are governed.

However, the indispensable quality of a relationship between social friends is total confidence in the integrity and character of the other. It is very important for them to share similar belief systems and principles if the relationship is to become close or elevated to a "best-friend" status. Best friends share their most private thoughts, ideas, fantasies and any secrets that they may have. They need the assurance that whatever they entrust into their friend's care will be guarded and protected with the utmost care. We have seen the effect of so-called friends violating the trust of someone who shared their innermost secrets. The person that violated the trust of another caused her "trusting friend" pain, embarrassment and probably a greater personal loss than anyone will ever know. True friends are committed to resisting the temptation to exploit each other by blatantly divulging confidential information. Violation of trust or breach of confidentiality destroys any ties that formally bound people together as friends. People expect such behavior from enemies but not from friends. *If my enemies were insulting me, I could endure it; if a foe were raising himself against me, I could hide from him. But it is you, a man like myself, my companion, my close friend, with whom I once enjoyed sweet fellowship* (Psm. 55:12-14). Betrayal by a friend is very hard to endure and could possibly affect the way a person approaches friendships for a long time to come. The feeling of assurance is replaced by a feeling of mistrust and suspicion. The freedom of communication for the joy of sharing with someone that was once trusted no longer exists. If a relationship between friends exists after one has violated the trust of another, it is taken to another level. What was once a close, trusted relationship usually becomes a superficial, guarded relationship.

Relationships between social friends are usually established because both people made a decision to enter into the relationship whether the friend is a family member or not. Because this is a relationship of choice, people usually choose to be loyal. Often people make the decision to take on friends because everyone <u>needs</u> someone that they can confide in, share the high and low points in their lives with, and to pray with. Friends must have common threads that connect them to each other mentally, socially and spiritually. Women need at least one female, confidential friend who is familiar enough with them to tell them when they are wrong and encourage them through trials and let them know that they are doing okay, woman-to-woman. There are some things, situations and consequences in life that are familiar to women that can only be understood by another woman. The same thing may be true for men as well. In many instances, God foresees the needs of His people to relate to someone who will not judge or condemn but will be there when the need arises. If believers pray for a friend with whom they can relate, He will send the right person along at the right time. He constantly extends the invitation for people to, *Cast your cares on the Lord and He will sustain you; He will never let the righteous fall*(Psm. 55:22).

There are many people who can identify with praying for a friend and getting the perfect answer to their prayer when they needed an answer the most. Sara Scott said she had longed for a female friend to laugh and share with for quite some time. She was an active member of a moderate church.

109

The people seemed nice enough but she did not feel very comfortable with any one person in particular. She had always admired an especially busy member, Jade, from a distance, but they had never really talked outside of church. Sara was reserved and always left immediately after service was over. One particular Sunday she came to the Morning Worship Services in emotional disarray. She was having some marital problems. She had left her family and friends to move across the country with her new husband. She had not met anyone that she felt comfortable enough with to share confidential information or even to socialize. She was surrounded by her husband's friends and relatives. She had prayed and prayed for God to send her a friend. She did not think God had heard her or she wasn't sure whether she was worthy of a friend.

That Sunday Morning as she sat on her pew, in so much emotional pain that she could not hold back the tears, the Spirit spoke to Jade whispering, "Go talk to Sara." Jade understood the Lord quite well but she did not think He meant right then. They were getting ready for altar prayer. Jade decided to talk with Sara after alter prayer. While she was at the altar, the voice of the Spirit repeated the command,"Go talk to Sara." By then everyone was returning to their seats. Jade looked around for Sara and she was no where to be seen. Fear of disobedience gripped Jade as she ran from the sanctuary to look for Sara. She spotted Sara in her car about to leave the parking lot. Jade, who was usually very composed and well-mannered, began to run towards Sara's car with her arms flailing, dress blowing in the wind, and hair going every sort of way. Sara did not know what was wrong with Jade but she stopped her car anyway. Jade walked to Sara's car and tapped on the window. When Sara let the window down just enough to hear what Jade had to say she was surprised, happy and out of sorts when Jade told her, "I do not know why I am here talking with you but the Spirit instructed me, more than once, to talk to you while we were in church." Sara was so relieved she began to weep bitterly. She shared a portion of her concerns with Jade and they prayed and exchanged telephone numbers. That was almost ten years ago. Jade and Sara have moved through many states during that period of time, but their friendship has just grown and continues to grow. Jade and Sara now live thousands and thousands of miles apart but the distance has not affected their friendship.

Sara and Jade have shared many wonderful shopping trips and other escapades that brought them joy. They have also shared many sorrows and disappointments down through the years. They have had disagreements and misunderstandings but they were always able to agree to disagree and move on. They still feel confident enough in each other's good character to share without holding back.

Some people take family and friends for granted. They rarely miss the people with whom they had close ties until something happens to sever the ties or separate them mind, spirit, soul and heart. Friendships must be nurtured if they are expected to grow. Some times very small misunderstandings can have an injurious affect on a relationship between friends and family. It is very important to work on relationships that matter and protect them from anything and anyone who may be injurious to the relationship. Sometimes people get close to others for the purpose of disrupting the harmony in some other relationship. Always get an understnading of your purpose and the purpose of others before taking them into your confidence. Never take anything, anyone or any situation involving those with whom you have ties that bind for granted. I did and had a most painful experience which fortunately, was short-lived.

I grew up with many sisters, a brother, and many nieces and nephews. When one sister moved from Memphis, Tennessee to Los Angeles, California, the entire family, including our parents, followed. I had never been separated from all my sisters at the same time in my entire life. About five years ago I got married. My husband's job was in Atlanta, Georgia. It did not occur to me that I was going to be leaving my family and friends after the wedding. I was so busy with wedding plans and moving household items that the separation never really came up.

My sister, Mary, and I lived on the same property along with two nieces, Shirley and Kelley. We could yell to each other from our windows. We had always been very close as sisters and as friends. We worked in similar professions and for the same establishment. We crossed each other's pathways in the hallways at work on many occasions. We had coffee together almost everyday. Sometimes we rode together going to work and other places. Our social lives were interlinked. I also lived very close to my other sisters. I often stopped by for a visit on my way home from work. I could walk into Kelley's house without ever having to go outside.

My husband, Larry, and I planned to leave the city the day after the wedding. We were loading the car and preparing to go to the airport when it hit me that I was leaving my house for the last time! It still had furniture that I was leaving for

Kelley. When it occurred to me that this was going to be a permanent separation of a few thousand miles, I got a lump in my throat and a feeling of dread in my gut. I was happy about my new life but I was devastated by having to give up portions of the old one. I could not bear the thought of saying good-by to my family so I tried to sneak away. Mary and Shirley looked out and saw us loading the car and came out to see us off. They were joined by Kelley. I tried hard to hold back the tears. As soon as we pulled away, I cried from the depths of my being. My husband was a good friend who understood my dilemma. After the honeymoon, he made arrangements for me to visit my family often during that first year. However, I was very lonely and was in need of a friend with whom I could connect mentally, socially and spiritually. I met many wonderful people and formed some very close ties with quite a few of them but that one "magnetic" connection had not occurred. I began to pray, and on a rainy night in December, a few months after our wedding, my prayers were answered. Larry and I were invited to a party at the home of Lisa and Earl Artis. Lisa and I did not seem to have much in common at first, but later when the party thinned out and we had an opportunity to talk, we both knew that we could be friends. We had kindred spirits. We became prayer partners as well. Our friendship is growing and developing as we grow and develop. We know that we can always depend on each other.

Although I am thousands of miles away from my sisters, my brother and my nieces and nephews, our relationships are still as close as ever. We visit each other occasionally. At the beginning of the year Mary had an extensive surgical procedure performed. I was convinced within my heart that no one could possibly take care of her like I could. I went there to care for her for two weeks. After two weeks had expired I was not satisfied that she was ready to be left alone. I was blessed and relieved when my husband permitted me to stay two more weeks to care for Mary. During that month we became closer than ever as friends. Although she required quite a bit of care and was not always feeling her best, we were able to spend some quality time together. Sometimes we laughed and talked into the night. We always had devotion together before we began our day. We resorted to some of our childhood days when we found silly things to laugh about. Together we were able to make the best out of an unfortunate situation. The ties that bind us together have never been loosened. They seemed to have grown tighter with time.

Many other types of relationships can evolve from friendship. Some friends decide to pool their resources and their energies and become partners in business. Some female/male friendships develop into intimate relationships and they decide to become partners for life. Friendship should be the beginning of most serious relationships that are expected to lead to marriage. It is an extra special blessing to be married to one's good friend.

Fiends who know the Lord, and who have friends who do not know the Lord should make a special effort to introduce them to the Lord. When friends are spiritually connected, it enhances their relationship. A personal relationship with the Lord is one that no one should take lightly or shun.

Chapter Six

THE ULTIMATE RELATIONSHIP

One thinks to oneself, " If the Lord gave me a sign
I would believe Him when He says , 'all the power is Mine.'

He said, "I can rearrange the heavens and overshadow the
sun.
I can raise the dead and command mountains to run.
I can give you everything you want and all that you see
but your soul would suffer because you never knew ME. "

Are you looking, waiting and hoping for an absolutely perfect relationship ? Are you looking for someone who will love you with a kind of love that you have never experienced before? Does there seem to be an empty space within your heart, spirit, and soul just yearning to be connected to something or someone really, really special? You may be among the masses who have wonderful, loyal friends, a loving family, an adoring spouse and many of the material things that you have dreamed of, but still feel that there is something more, something missing. Do you still seem to have a longing deep within your soul that you cannot put your finger on? All that you yearn or long for is possible for you today! You will not have to change very many things in your present lifestyle, unless that is your desire. You won't have to give up your friends, your family, or your spouse to achieve fulfillment. Your material possessions will be yours to keep. If you are single, this applies to you also. You can find everything you need to reach fulfillment in any special area of your life. I can introduce you to the Creator and Founder of love who can fulfill every desire of your heart! Some of you may have already met Him but you may need to renew the acquaintance. Others may have an interpersonal relationship with Him already and are sharing His purpose for their lives. He is beautiful from the inside out. He is kind, gentle and not hard to get along with at all. He is concerned about everything that concerns you, every minute of every day. He is the Master of wisdom, knowledge and understanding. In fact He knows absolutely everything. He will be delighted to answer you whenever you want to come to Him for advice, questions, on any kind of problem. He is more powerful than anyone else any where, so He is more than capable of taking good care of you all the time. He will protect you so that nothing can harm you. You will never have to look for Him because He is everywhere all at once. I tell you, He is just perfect. He wants to establish an interpersonal relationship with you right now. He promises to be there for you always under any conditions in any kind of weather, ..."*And surely I am with you always, to the very end of the age"*(Mat 28:20). He will never, never leave or forsake you, even if you turn and walk away from Him. He will be there waiting with open arms to welcome you, and will receive you back when you return. He will even watch over you while you are away from Him, but He will not interfere in your life, unless you specifically ask Him to.

His love offers much more than an expression of adoration

when you have done something that pleases Him. It offers more than an intense feeling of affection based on familiar ties. His love is alive, active and powerful. It cannot be fully explained, but once you have experienced it you will know that no other love can compare to His love. It is powerful enough to make you change your mind about many things. It brings about a change in your attitude that can have a positive affect on your heart, soul, and spirit. This love is given freely whether you deserve it or not. *He demonstrated His love towards us in this: While we were still sinners, Christ died for us* (Ro. 5:8). Actually, no one deserved this kind of love but because of His love, grace, mercy, and the a*bundant provision of grace and of the gift of righteousness can reign in your life through the one man Jesus Christ* (Ro. 5:17). Grace is the kindness by which God bestows favors and blessings on the ill-deserving and grants them pardon for their offenses. His love will never be withdrawn from you under any circumstances. It is unconditional and eternal. His love expresses some of His characteristic traits, interests and plans that He wants to share with you.

His love is *patient and kind* because He is patient and kind. When you receive His love, you will have the capacity to endure hardships without murmuring and complaining. You will also be able to bear delays without becoming frustrated. Understanding, friendliness and warm-heartiness will also be made available to you. His love *always protects, always hopes, always trusts and always preserves.* Because His love represents the essence of Him, it can also give you some insights into how great He is. His love has the power to keep you safe from the snares that are set for you in the material world.

When you open your heart and this love flows in, it brings the assurance and total confidence in His integrity that can cast out fears and make you feel safe. *There is no fear in love. Perfect love drives out fear, because fear has to do with punishment. The one who fears is not made perfect in love* (IJn. 4:18). You will also be able to wish for things, ask for things and expect the desires of your transformed heart to come to pass. His love is always consistent with His character.

These are some of the things that His love may change about you to make your spirit correspond to His spirit. His love *does not envy or boast.* The attitudes that illicit these responses are not associated with Him. When you decide to establish a relationship with Him, you should not have resentful desires to possess anything that belongs to someone else. You will learn to be content under any circumstances. His love can motivate you to renew your mind. *You will not have to conform to the patterns of the material world any longer but you can be transformed by the renewing of your mind* (Ro. 12:2). The desire to brag or speak excessively about your material possessions, accomplishments and natural abilities should not enter your mind. Once your mind has been renewed you will know that everything comes from Him because *All good gifts come from above* (Jas. 1:17).

He is the author and founder of peace and harmony that bring calmness to the spirit and He wants to share those qualities with you. His love is in no way *self-seeking and it does not anger easily.* There are things that some people still want to do that could put them in harm's way, this may make Him angry but He is usually long-suffering with everyone. His love should motivate you to align your interests and concerns with His. It is in your best interest not to harbor feelings of hostility, indignation, or anything that can prevent you from controlling your responses to negative impressions. When His love has been transplanted in your heart, you should not *delight in evil but rejoice in truth.* One of the most profound things about His love is that it *never fails.* It is always effective and it is always sufficient in quality and quantity. (Italicized phrases about love from I Cor. 13:4-8).

You must know who He is by now, but I want you to really be able to recognize Him, so I will give you a little more information on His character and abilities to perform. The prophet Isaiah says, *He sits enthroned above the circle of the earth, and its people are like grasshoppers. He stretches out the heavens like a canopy, and spreads them out like a tent to live in. He brings out the starry host one by one and calls them each by name. Because of His great power and mighty strength, not one of them is missing*(Is. 40:22,26). He is one great Spirit; however, He and His Son, Jesus, and the Holy Spirit, are three distinct personalities that function in a united manner to bring about His purpose and His plan. Their purpose and plan for your life include, redemption, abundant life and eternal life with Christ. All three Personalities are eager for you to establish a relationship with them. They have the power to transplant their divine attributes within your heart and affect a change that will be consistent with their nature. They do not make any alterations to your natural spirit. In a

119

mystical way that only they know, they insert an entirely new divine Spirit within your innermost being. Redemption denotes release, or freedom, by payment of a price. Christ is man's redeemer. He paid the price on the cross for human redemption. When anyone accepts Him, Satan's power and dominion are broken, giving redeemed people the power to lead new lives. *Therefore, if anyone is in Christ, he is a new creation, the old has gone, and the new has come (2 Cor. 5:17)!*

The idea to establish the relationship does not originate within you. Jesus explains that, *"No one can come to Me unless the Father who sent Me draws him and I will raise him up on the last day."* (Jn. 6:44) The Father and Son are working together to fulfill their promise of eternal life with them. However, you must make the decision to open the door of your heart and permit Him to come in and communicate with you. Jesus is still saying, *"Here I am! I stand at the door and knock. If anyone hears my voice and opens the door I will come in and eat with him and he with Me"* (Rev. 3:20). This is how that works. God has already devised a plan for everyone to be drawn to His Son Jesus. He will teach them whatever they need to know and enable them to come when He draws them. This is done by the Holy Spirit who is at work on your behalf at the command of the Father. An experience that you cannot adequately explain will begin to take place inside you. It is a total spiritual experience, so only others who are in a personal relationship with God will understand. Like all other life experiences, the decision to come or not to come when you hear the Voice within your heart will determine whether you will experience the most wonderful love in the world. God loves you more than you have the capacity to comprehend! This is how much He loves you right now. Try very hard to digest this. *This is love: Not that we loved God, but that He loved us and sent His Son as an atoning sacrifice for our sins*(Is. 4:10). God's holiness, which is another one of His attributes, demands punishment for mankind's sins. Out of Love, He sent His son to the cross to die and become a substitute for your sins and the sins of every one of His creatures. If you ever visit the cross where Jesus laid His life on the line for you, you may never view life the same again.

First Jesus was betrayed by one of His disciples. *Now Judas, who betrayed Him, knew the place* (Jn. 18:2). You must know how it feels to be betrayed by someone you love. Then His friend, Peter, whom Jesus had chosen to feed His sheep, denied his association with Jesus while Jesus was being questioned by the Roman officials. *"You are not one of His disciples are you?"* *the girl at the door asked Peter. He replied, "I am not"* (Jn. 18:17). The very people He came to pardon condemned Him. *They shouted, "Take Him away! Take Him away! Crucify Him"* (Jn. 19:15). *So the soldiers took charge of Jesus. Carrying His own cross, He went to a place of the Skull (which in Aramaic is called Golgotha). Here they crucified Him.* He watched from the cross w*hen the soldiers took His clothes and divided them in four shares. When He saw His mother there and the disciple whom He loved standing nearby, He said to His mother,"Dear woman, here is your Son," and to the disciple,"Here is your Mother." Later, knowing that all was completed, and so that the Scripture would be fulfilled , Jesus said, "I am thirsty." A jar*

121

of wine vinegar was there, so they soaked a sponge in it, put the sponge on a stalk of hyssop plant, and lifted it to Jesus' lips. When He had received the drink, Jesus said,"It is finished," one of the soldiers pierced Jesus' side with a spear, bringing a sudden flow of blood and water (Jn. 19: 16, 23, 26, 28, 29,34). This represents only a part of the agony Jesus underwent so that you could be reconciled to God through the shedding of His blood. Before Jesus was handed over to the soldiers to be crucified, Pilate had Him flogged. The soldiers *stripped Him and put a scarlet robe on Him, and twisted together a crown of thorns and set it on His head. They spit on Him and took the staff and struck Him on the head again and again* (Mat. 27: 26, 28-30). Floggings were extremely brutal. Sometimes victims actually died from the agony of the floggings.

When you establish a relationship with God, your sins are turned away from you and directed towards Christ. Everyone will have an equal opportunity to meet Him and decide whether or not they want to establish an interpersonal relationship with Him. You are probably wondering,"Why did Jesus subject Himself to such humiliation and physical pain?" He did it because of His great love, and His desire to restore the personal relationship man had with God before a decision was made to sin. The shedding of purified blood was the only way to bring mankind together in a union of peace with God and others. However, it was the resurrection of Jesus that completed God's perfect plan of salvation. Jesus died the agonizing death as an example for redeemed mankind to follow. He was crucified in the flesh literally so that You and I could be crucified in the flesh spiritually. The painful experience prior to Jesus' crucifixion is a reminder to every believer of the great price Jesus paid for his/her redemption. It is also a reminder to every non-believer that because of God's grace, he/she can enter into a relationship with Jesus based on the provisions He has already made for redemption. The choice is this: Either accept the free gift of love or reject the invitation to "come." To accept the offer that cost so much has many rewards, which include peace, according to John 14:27, *"Peace I leave with you; my peace I give you. I do not give peace as the world gives. Do not let your hearts be troubled,"* said Jesus. You get citizenship in the Spiritual world, *"They are not of the world even as I am not of it,"* said *Jesus. "But our citizenship is in heaven"* (Jn. 17:16 & Phil. 3:20). Christians are fully involved in the world but their interests are dominated by things in heaven. Their focus should never move away from the cross which reminds them of their pledge to crucify their flesh. Christians also get indispensable protection at the request of Jesus to the Father. *"My prayer is not that you take them out of the world but that you protect them from the evil one"* (Jn. 17:15). There are so many more priceless benefits for those who choose to enter into a relationship with God through Jesus Christ, but you only experience them after you enter into the ultimate relationship. The ultimate relationship can be likened to an insurance policy in one way, but it is very different in another way. You can realize that there are benefits that can be made available to you but you only get to reap them *after* you have agreed to purchase the policy and actually make a payment. Jesus has paid the full amount of the premium on your behalf. All you have to do is accept the free gift that He is offering you and read the terms of the agreement! If you choose by your will, to reject the offer of the free gift of redemption, you are making a decision to accept the consequences of that decision. The consequences of rejection include: denunciation on the day of judgment in accordance with the teachings of Jesus. *"Whoever disowns me before men, I will disown him before my Father in Heaven. But I tell you that it will be more bearable for Sodom on the day of judgment than for you"* (Mat. 10:34 & 11:24). God gives gifts of love because of His grace and not because of our merit. However, He takes rejection of His Son's crucifixion experience seriously. What you are saying, in essence, when you choose to reject the sacrifice God made for you through Jesus is; "The horrible pre-crucifixion torment and the humiliation that Jesus suffered on the cross was of no value to me." Jesus will say to you, *"Depart from me, you who are cursed into the eternal fire prepared for the devil and his angels"* (Mat. 25:41). If you are being deceived by believing that a loving God would not sentence people to burn in the eternal fires of hell, you are not altogether wrong. He does not sentence anyone to such a horrible eternity. Each person chooses good relationships and bad relationships. Each person's consequences will be in accordance with the decisions he or she has made.

The Father, the Son and the Holy Spirit want this relationship to come to pass. Jesus has removed all the barriers by defeating the influences of the devil and his evil spirits. He offers you the same authority He gave the disciples. *"I have given you authority [power]) to trample on snakes and scorpions [evil spirits] and to overcome all the power of the enemy [the devil himself] and nothing will harm you* (Lk. 10:19). However, this authority will only be given to those who admit that they need to overpower the influences that the evil spirits have over their unaltered spirit.

This is truly the ultimate relationship. It is the one that will prove to be the most significant relationship you will ever enter into, and it is available to you. The ties that bind you to the Lord can never be severed once the transformation has taken place within your heart, soul, and spirit. It will bring joy and not misery to the soul, now and even when the soul is disembodied. That fact alone is enough to rejoice about. Eternal life will be spent with the Father, the Son, and the Holy Spirit where, *No eye has seen, no ear has heard, no mind has conceived what God has prepared for those who love Him* (I Cor. 2:9). Do not be among those who allow the enemy to deceive their minds. The offer of redemption and eternal life is real. You will benefit from the relationship every day while you are alive, and even after your mortal body no longer exists. However, it is important to understand that the decision to accept or reject the love gift of redemption must be made before physical death occurs to reap the benefit of eternal life. Remember the rich man who died but was still tortured day and night in the fires of hell? He failed to make provisions for his soul while he was alive.

When people engage in personal relationships, they want to enjoy each other's company by spending time together. A relationship between you and God through Jesus connects you to the Father by the blood. A kinship is developed which makes you family. It will take time, effort and energy to maintain this relationship. You become like a brother or sister to Jesus! God becomes a nurturing Father who uses His word to instruct you on family rules and regulations. As His child, you should take the time to learn the teachings of Jesus. God has everything that you will ever need to develop into the person He created you to become. As you are being developed to conform to His image, you should learn that how you develop depends on your obedience to the teachings of Jesus.

Your training as a new creation in Christ will be superimposed on what you already know. It will be your decision to apply the teachings to your day-to-day life experiences. The greatest lesson a child of God's has to learn is the lesson of obedience. Obedience comes with total submission. God will not take second place to anyone or anything else in your life. If there are people or things that are more important to you than God, He perceives them as idols or foreign gods. *He is a holy God; He is a jealous God. Throw away the foreign gods that are among you and yield your hearts to the Lord* (Jos. 24:19 &24).

He is not jealous in the natural sense. It is not in His nature to be resentful or become a rival for your love and affections. He is intolerant of disloyalty and is very protective of you. He knows what all your tomorrows hold, when you are obedient and also when you are disobedient. When you enter into a relationship with Him, you become His very own possession. Your way of showing gratitude, reverent respect, and love for Him is through obedience. After all, everything you are, own and do is because of Him. Obedience is not required to show you how much power He has. He does not necessarily want to restrict you. He wants you to choose to follow Him because He knows where He is going. He wants to make sure you get where you were created to be without encountering harm. Obedience is required as a protective measure as well as a means of blessing you. Whatever and whomever you place before Him becomes a god in His eyesight. When you choose to serve other gods with worshipful reverence, it means that you are disloyal to Him. You may subconsciously serve friends, children, spouses, or material things with more worshipful reverence than you serve the Lord. Jesus says, *"Anyone who loves his father or mother more than Me is not worthy of Me; and anyone who loves his son or daughter more than me is not worthy of Me"*(Mat. 10: 37). Part of the new nurturing process is to learn the teachings of Jesus so that you will worship and serve the Lord with gladness. After all, He has made provisions for you to have absolutely everything that you need. No one else can or will ever do that for you.

Jesus came down from heaven and underwent a lot of agony on the cross so that you could enter into a relationship with the Father through Him. He wants to make you new from the inside out. The relationship between yourself and Him unites you in a mystic union, whereby He becomes a part of you and you become a part of Him, similar to the unity that comes with marriage but much, much deeper than that. *All this is from God who reconciled us to Himself through Christ....not counting our sins against us* (2 Cor. 5:19). When you choose to live in the newness of life, you will begin to experience the evidence of God's love, grace, mercy, and other fruits of His goodness. The more you learn about Jesus, the more you will want to know. The more you apply what you

127

learn, the more you will understand how you can benefit from this divine relationship. When a change takes place within your heart, you will have an impending desire to be obedient as well as worship and serve the Lord with all your heart, all your soul and all your understanding. Once you fully understand what it means to be a new creation in Christ, you will look at His commands in a different light. When you see that obedience is required to reap many of the benefits, you will search the Scriptures to see what He has made available to you and the conditions under which you can inherit what is available. Such teachings as, "*If you obey My commands you will remain in My love. I have told you this so that My joy may be in you and your joy may be complete*"(Jn. 15: 10-11).

If you want to remain in Him and to have complete joy, you will begin to look for the things He commands. He has put forth every effort to make relating to Him easy for you. You will not have to look far. In the very next verse He says, "*This is my command, 'Love each other as I have loved you.'* You already know how His love works from the previous phrases on divine love. He even tells you the conditions under which your prayers will be answered! "*If you remain in Me and My words remain in you, ask whatever you wish and it will be given to you*" (Jn. 15:7). Many of the Biblical references relating to obedience, as a means of acquiring some of your benefits, clearly defines what you must do in order to make things happen for you. It is impossible to live in the newness of life and have enough faith to move mountains, cast mulberry trees into oceans, and pray in God's will, without knowing the teachings of Jesus. Compare the granting of your wishes to shopping for the things you need and desire. These things are available to you but you cannot benefit from them until you get up, go out, and purchase them. Some action is required on your part. Maintaining a relationship requires serious thoughts, decision making, and action on your part. Keeping the ultimate relationship intact requires nothing less. Once you decide to make the teachings of Jesus your very own, they are your possessions to use so that you can experience life to its fullest. Your love and your faith will increase. Look what you can do with a little faith. *"If you have faith as small as a mustard seed, you can say to this mulberry bush, be rooted up and planted in the sea and it will obey you"* (Lk. 17:6). Are you asking,"Where do I get faith from?" *Consequently, faith comes from hearing the message, the message is heard through the word of Christ* (Ro. 10:17). It is all there for you. Now think of what you can do with a lot of faith!

Everyone has empty spaces within their innermost beings that long to be filled. Some of those spaces long to be filled by relationships that many people have never experienced before. Many spouses are together physically but they may not be mentally and spiritually connected. Both partners may long for a mental and spiritual connection to fill the emptiness within each of them. Children, who have never experienced love and acceptance from their parents, may long to experience love and acceptance from them. Even people who have never shared their innermost secrets with anyone may long for a close friend to interact with. Each person may think, "If only I could have that one special relationship, I would be satisfied." The empty spaces within a person's inner most parts cannot always be filled by relationships with other human beings. Sometimes the longing may be for a

129

relationship with God. The space within that is reserved for God cannot be filled by anything or anyone else. Nothing or no one else can come close. Until the one significant relationship between you and God is established, there will always be an empty space within your innermost being. You will never fully appreciate the excellency of His power as He moves through the world that He has created, but once you know Him you will learn to respect and appreciate it.

Once this ultimate relationship has been established, your vision, desires, disposition and appreciation for the power of God changes. When you can perceive his greatness within your spirit, you will worship and reverence Him in awe and wonderment. The feelings, expressions and experiences just grow and grow. I know that God was and is awesome and powerful with the ability to be everywhere all at once. I also know that He knows everything about everyone and everything. However, He showed me a display of His powers in a way that I shall never forget. Even as I attempt to share the experience with you, I know that words cannot fully capture what I witnessed that night.

It was the last week of July, 1998. My husband, Larry, and I were in Memphis, Tennessee at a convention. We had taken a friend home who lived in a development in a remote area of the city. As soon as we began to drive back to our hotel, a fierce storm arose. It was already past midnight and the area was not that well lit to begin with. Suddenly the skies became very dark and a torrential flow of rain soon followed. Visibility was very bad. Every now and then the skies would light up with flashes of lightning and the earth was filled with loud roars and claps of thunder. The flashes of lightning and roars of thunder became more frequent and more intense. I saw furrows of lightning that made wide pathways with branch like extensions of bright white rays of light, surrounded by hues of yellow that lit up the skies like it was mid-day. As the branches of light formed from the huge pathway of light, in what seemed like grooves of excitement before my eyes, I knew that there was enough power in the skies before me to burn the whole city to the ground if the lightning had touched down anywhere on earth. Instead, everything became illuminated for a limited length of time. Some of the channels of light seemed to just hang in the skies. Others danced around in the skies, jumping around from place to place before God gathered them up and returned them to their hiding place. There were times when one pathway of lightning seemed to superimpose itself on an existing furrow. The power of God was both frightening and awesome. We had to drive very slowly because of the sheets of rain that poured down from the heavens. I felt and saw a small portion of the power of the Lord as, *The clouds poured down water, the skies resounded with thunder and His arrows flashed back and forth. His lightning lit up the world*(Psm. 77:17). It must have taken us more than an hour to get back to our hotel. Under normal conditions, it would have taken fifteen minutes. The display of power in the skies was more brilliant than any laser show could ever match. Larry had worked as a meteorologist some time ago. He said that he had never witnessed such a display of lightning in his entire life. He informed me that there was enough power in the heavens to burn up two or three worlds if all that lightning had touched down at one time. That further magnified the power of God in my mind, soul and spirit. God was in complete control of the lightning and thunder, and He kept us, and others who were not aware of what was going on in their world, safe from any harm.

A relationship with God can enhance every other relationship you enter into or already have. God can be a business partner, a college professor, a friend, and He can even take the place of parents and spouses. He knows everything there is to know about everything and everyone. He can advise and guide you in business and in whatever profession you choose to work. He can make your job easier and more pleasant if you invite Him to share with you. He can be a really, really good friend because He will always be with you and He can comfort you when you need comforting and be there for you when you are lonely. He is faithful, loyal and a perfect confidant. He will listen to every thing you want to say to Him and He will never violate your trust in Him. He will never tell anyone anything that you tell Him. He will even intervene if you ask Him. Invite Him to share in your relationship with your spouse, your children, your parents and everyone that you hold dear. He is interested in every one of your interests, activities and purposes. If you invite Him to share in all of your relationships, He will tell you what to avoid. He knows where each stumbling block has been placed along the pathway of your life now, and forever. He will tell you what to do, what to say and how to behave in every situation, but only if you ask Him. You can take Him anywhere you go. He is a perfect gentleman. His character is above reproof. He will never embarrass you.

Your relationship with Him should be in accordance with the Golden Rule. Relate to Him in the same manner you want Him to relate to You. If you love Him, you will be compelled to keep His commands. He will return your love by making sure you enjoy all the benefits that are available to you. This should not be a one-sided relationship. Just as you get on the telephone and talk with your friends and put forth an effort to attend affairs with them, you should share equal time with the Lord. Call Him up and talk with Him. Put forth an effort to enter into His presence regularly and do not be in a hurry to leave from His presence. Embrace Him (by embracing His word) with the love and affection that you embrace your loved ones. Do it often just because you love Him. He lives in your spirit. Every time you feed your natural body, give some thought to how and what you feed your spirit. Give Him an opportunity to become Lord of your life. When you make Him Lord, the affects of the ultimate relationship will become intense and more fulfilling than anything you have ever experienced. To make Him Lord, you must choose, by your will, to submit to His power and authority in everything you do, think and say. As Lord, He becomes the Master who will teach you doctrines and direct every portion of your life. He also accepts responsibility for you as well. Remember, He knows everything there is to know about you, including your today and tomorrow. He wants you to fulfill the purpose for which you were created. When you *know* that your life is being lived in accordance with a divine plan and that you are in God's will, you will have a joy and a type of peace that surpasses all human understanding. *The peace of God, which transcends all understanding, will guard your hearts and minds in Christ Jesus (Php. 4:7).*

Yes, this is the ultimate relationship and it just continues to get better. It was designed to enhance and overshadow all other relationships. If the Ultimate relationship preceded all other relationships, people could avoid many disappointments, disagreements, pain, anger, and many other feelings that arise when wrong, unfruitful decisions are made. God really, really loves you and He has a wonderful plan for your life. The ultimate relationship will last throughout this lifetime and beyond. All the things you seek from others, like peace different from any other peaceful situation, and joy that remains within your heart under any circumstances, can be found in God. Even if you choose to reject His love offering of redemption, He will not take His love away from you. In fact, He continues to offer His love gift to anyone who has the faith, courage and desire to accept it. Jesus is still saying to you, *Here I am! I stand at the door and knock. If anyone hears my voice and opens the door, I will come in and eat with him and he with Me"* (Rev. 3:20). He will accept you just the way you are. His love and acceptance are unconditional, they are only portions of the rewards and benefits that you will receive in this life and the life to come. These things make this relationship so much more unique and more fulfilling than other relationships. It will be far different from any other relationship you have known or will ever know.

A relationship with God, through Jesus, is easy. You can enter into this ultimate relationship with God by believing that God is who He says He is in the Scriptures and receiving the free gift of redemption, that has already been purchased with the blood of Jesus. *If you confess with your mouth, "Jesus is*

Lord," and believe in your heart that God raised Him from the dead, you will be saved (Ro. 10:9).

Epilogue

There will never be a perfect relationship between mortal, human beings. Even the relationship human beings enter into with the Lord is not without some imperfections, because people are not without imperfections. People are entering into a relationship with a perfect God, hoping to become like Him. However, the standards of all healthy relationships were founded by God. The principles governing healthy relationships arise from godly qualities like trust, honesty, commitment, respect and loyalty. These are the qualities that constitute good, moral character. Intimate relationships should be governed by the same standards as all other relationships, but they are on a different level because people usually become more emotionally involved in affairs of the heart. Marital relationships, and the relationships leading up to marriage, should be separated from general relationships. Intimate relationships should be given special time and attention. So watch for the next book, coming soon, called, *Until Death Do Us Part*. The following is a brief synopsis of *Until Death Do Us Part*.

Girls begin to prepare for that walk down the aisle in their white lace, with promises of a" life happily ever after," from the cradle. Boys begin to learn how to "sow their wild oats" before making a commitment to marriage. The dream of an ideal marriage is not always consistent with the day-to-day activities involved in building a healthy relationship, that can last. While there will probably be many similarities, interests, activities and purpose, couples should be prepared for many differences of opinion and many other differences that they will encounter when they must go to bed and wake up to the same person every single day.

· People should learn to enjoy life before marriage and pay particular attention to what that life entails. It is important for couples to make sure they are "through being single" before they make a life- time commitment to be with someone *Until Death Do Us Part*. Single life is not just a waiting period until the right person comes along. It should not be spent waiting, hoping and searching for that perfect, special mate. It is a uniquely special time for explorations, growing and developing. It is a time for thinking and being selfish in thoughts and activities. It is a time that should be devoted to being single. This is the time for people to begin being the best that they can be. It is the*only* time people have to be individuals. Sometimes during the course of self-discovery and exploration of all of your possibilities, you might learn that marriage may not be for you, or you could discover your partner for life in some of the most unusual places. You may also discover that there is a time for everything and everything has an allocated season. You should discover how wise it would be to wait until your *season* for marriage arrives.

The courtship period in a pre-marital relationship is almost as important as the marriage. During this period people should really get to know the person with whom they are contemplating spending the remaining days of their lives. There will not always be many changes in the interests and purpose of a person after the wedding. Marriage does not come equipped with a magic wand that will change a toad into a prince, a turtle into a princess, or a sow into a silk purse.

Whatever one sees and experiences in a courtship is usually a sneak preview of what married life will be like for him/her.

Wedding vows made before God and man go far beyond the *"To have and to hold"* phase. Marriages often go through the *"through sickness and in health.... and for better or worse"* phase many times over. Think long and hard *before* you make a commitment. Will you still have the wedding day glow and be able to keep your promise if some of the better days become worst than anything you have imagined or experienced? Worst days in a marriage go beyond lack of finances, different schedules, or even minor illnesses. Marriage is an agreement between two people to put forth their best effort to maintain unity under some trying circumstances. It is an agreement made before God and man. Some of the terms of this agreement are enforceable by law. Read between the lines before signing the contract! It is designed to last longer than a good car and an even better house. People spend time inspecting cars and houses before they make a decision to purchase either or both of them. They read the large print, the small print and between each line before signing the contracts. If they are not sure of the terms of the agreement, they may seek legal assistance before signing the contract. Marriage should be *Until Death Do Us Part*. Think long and hard about the agreement before signing the contract..

BOOK AVAILABLE THROUGH
Milligan Books
An Imprint Of Professional Business
Consulting Service

Affairs Of The Heart, Soul, And Spirit $11.95

Order Form

Milligan Books
1425 West Manchester, Suite B,
Los Angeles, California 90047
(323) 750-3592

Mail Check or Money Order to:
Milligan Books

Name _____ Date _____

Address _____

City_____ State _____ Zip Code_____

Day telephone _____

Evening telephone_____

Book title _____

Number of books ordered ___ Total cost .... $_____

Sales Taxes (CA Add 8.25%) .... $_____

Shipping & Handling $3.00 per book .... $_____

Total Amount Due..$_____

· Check   · Money Order   Other Cards _____

· Visa   · Master Card   Expiration Date _____

Credit Card No. _____

Driver's License No. _____

_____   _____

Signature   Date